MW01060267

Also by the Author

The Erin O'Reilly Mysteries
Black Velvet
Irish Car Bomb
White Russian (coming soon)

The Clarion Chronicles
Ember of Dreams

Irish Car Bomb

The Erin O'Reilly Mysteries
Book Two

Steven Henry

Clickworks Press • Baltimore, MD

First publication: Clickworks Press, 2018
Release: CWP-EOR2-INT-P.IS-1.3.2

Sign up for updates, deals, and exclusive sneak peeks at clickworkspress.com/join.

ISBN-10: 1-943383-38-3
ISBN-13: 978-1-943383-38-2

For the dedicated members of Precinct 8: The diehards, Ingrid, David, and Justin, who went the distance, beginning to end; and those who joined us for part of the journey: Hilary, Bridget, Mark, and Ben. This story exists because of all of you.

Irish Car Bomb

Pour 1 pint of Irish Stout into a pub glass. Float ½ shot of Irish whiskey on top of ½ shot of Irish Cream in a shot glass. Drop the shot glass into the stout. Serve straight up, without ice. Drink quickly.

Warning: *This drink name is considered offensive in many places, especially in Ireland. It is a reference to the infamous car-bombings which were common during the Troubles. Ordering it in an Irish pub can be tactless at best.*

Chapter 1

Erin O'Reilly sighed. She had a shield on her belt and a Glock automatic on her hip, but after eleven years of working Patrol, she wasn't used to going to work without the uniform. It wasn't until this moment, her first day on her new job, that she'd realized all the little rituals she'd gotten used to performing at the start of a shift. She'd always adjusted her hat to just the right angle, and made sure the shield on her chest was perfectly aligned. The uniform centered her, made her feel like part of a team. Now she was bareheaded, her hair in a ponytail, wearing a modest, professional blouse, black slacks, and sensible boots, the soles cheating an extra two inches onto her five-foot-six frame. Even the shield she carried was different. Cops talked about getting their gold shield, the mark of a detective, but now that she had it, she wasn't even sure she felt like a cop anymore.

"I don't know about this, Rolf," she said to her partner.

Rolf wagged his tail. He wasn't worried, but then, he never had to think about what to wear. The German Shepherd was always ready to go.

Erin shook her head and let herself out. Though she'd gotten up early for her usual morning run with Rolf, she didn't have time to hang around mooning. She hadn't been able to find a place in Manhattan, so she was still living in her old studio apartment in Queens. That meant a daily commute into the big city. Just another thing to get used to.

She walked briskly to the nearest Number Seven Line subway station, Rolf trotting at her side. She carried a fold-together file box with some supplies she thought she might need. It was a straight shot in to Grand Central Station, then an easy walk to Precinct 8.

The subway ride gave her plenty of time to worry about other things than her wardrobe. She was a newly-minted detective, going to work in an unfamiliar precinct with a bunch of cops she'd never met. She had no idea what to expect. At least Captain Holliday had seemed friendly enough and her dad, a retired cop, had only positive things to say about him.

"He's good police," Sean O'Reilly had said when she'd told him about her transfer to Holliday's new Major Crimes unit. "Totally honest, a real straight shooter. He came up the right way, from Patrol through Homicide. Just do your job, do it well, and you'll be fine. If you're one of his, he'll have your back."

"He can't be worse than Spinelli," Erin said to Rolf, remembering the Queens Homicide detective she'd made an enemy for life by taking the credit for his biggest case.

Rolf cocked his head at her. He didn't understand much human speech, but that didn't stop him from trying.

"We're gonna be fine, boy," she said, scratching him behind the ears. But she didn't even sound convincing to herself. It was normal to partner a new transfer with one of the old hands in a department, so the new girl could learn the ropes. But Erin didn't want any partner but Rolf. She'd had some friction with police guys before, especially the ones who assumed having a female partner meant extracurricular favors.

The train finally pulled into Grand Central. Erin was familiar with the station. Her parents had taken her into Manhattan dozens of times while she was growing up. But somehow, even when she'd been a little girl, it had never looked quite so big. She reminded herself that first-day jitters were the most common thing in the world and that she was a veteran cop, not a rookie.

Her shift started at eight. She glanced at her watch as she came up on the precinct. She had almost fifteen minutes to spare, having given herself a cushion for the first day. The building didn't look like much, five stories of beat-up brick built over a basement garage. It was overdue for a renovation, but that was typical of every police station she'd ever been in.

Erin swallowed, took a deep breath, and climbed the stairs.

*   *   *

The duty sergeant at the front desk raised an eyebrow. "Help you, ma'am?"

"I'm looking for Major Crimes," she said.

"And you are?"

"O'Reilly, transfer from Queens 116."

"Okay, sign in," the sergeant said. "Shield?"

She flashed her ID and signed the spiral pad.

"Welcome to the Old Eightball, O'Reilly. You want the second floor." He angled a thumb. "Stairs and elevator."

Riding the elevator to the second floor would be ridiculous. Erin took the stairs.

She and Rolf emerged into a wide-open space. The second floor of the precinct had structural columns dotted throughout. The only walls were around the captain's office, the break room, and the bathroom. She saw a handful of desks with outdated, boxy computer monitors, a whiteboard, a copy machine, a fax, and a meeting table. The table and desks were scarred and scratched. No one was in sight.

"I guess they don't get here early," Erin said. She glanced into the break room. There was a coffee machine, which was good, and a pot of coffee already made up, which was even better, but the couch and coffee table were just about the most disreputable pieces of furniture she'd ever seen.

Her police instincts nagged at her. If a pot of coffee was brewed up, then someone had beaten her here. Where was he, or she?

Even as she thought it, she heard the sound of a faucet from the direction of the bathroom. She turned in time to see Captain Holliday come through the door, drying his hands.

"O'Reilly," he said. "Morning. Glad you're here."

"Thank you, sir," she said, stiffening her spine. "Am I early?"

He smiled through his mustache. "Far from it, Detective. I'm sorry about this, but it looks like you're going to have one of those first days."

"What do you mean, sir?"

"You'll have to learn on the job," he said. "The call from Dispatch beat you here by a quarter of an hour. When the call comes in, the cavalry rides out. You'll need to meet your unit on site."

"We've got a case?" she asked. Her heart was suddenly pounding, her jitters forgotten with the rush of excitement that always came when she went into action.

"Apparently a man got blown up on his way to work this morning," the captain said dryly.

"Blown up, sir?"

"Car bomb," Holliday said. "Don't ask me, I wasn't there. You'd best get moving. Call Dispatch. They'll tell you where to go. When you get to the scene, ask for Lieutenant Webb."

Erin hurriedly laid her box of office supplies on the most

deserted-looking desk and went straight back outside. Rolf followed.

She'd just gotten out the door of the precinct house and was reaching for a shoulder radio she wasn't wearing when she remembered she didn't have a squad car, either. Mentally kicking herself, she used her phone to call in to Dispatch to get the address. She could've gone back inside and asked Holliday how to access the motor pool, but time was ticking at the crime scene and she was already embarrassed. She'd improvise. The important thing was to get there. She hailed a cab.

* * *

The site of the blast was an underground parking garage off Second Avenue, between 24th and 25th Street. Erin paid the cabbie and took in the scene. She was definitely at the right location. Squad cars had cordoned off the garage and a large number of bystanders were milling around at a respectful distance. As she and Rolf approached, she heard a woman say, "I'm sure I saw the bomb squad. Is it terrorists, do you think?"

"Muslims, probably," her companion replied. "Al Qaeda."

Erin inwardly rolled her eyes at the rubberneckers as she passed. The apartment complex was middle-class, about fifteen floors, built of tan bricks with a row of restaurants at ground level. There were no signs of structural damage, no clouds of smoke pouring out of the garage. If this had been a bomb, it hadn't been too big. Going out on a speculative limb, she was willing to bet it didn't indicate a massive terrorist strike on New York City.

She showed her shield to the uniforms at the entrance and identified herself. They stepped aside and she and Rolf went down the ramp. Partway down, the dog abruptly froze in his "alert" posture. A moment later, Erin smelled it too. Rolf was trained in explosives detection, and something had definitely blown up not long before. There was a smell of smoke, burnt fuel, and charred metal.

A small group of men and women were standing around the wreckage of the car. There was a big guy with a broken nose and a blond buzz cut. Next to him was a man in a trench coat, holding an unlit cigarette. A woman with hair dyed electric blue at the tips glanced up, saw Erin, and smiled a little nervously at her. Another woman in a white lab coat was kneeling next to something black and smoldering. The smell told Erin she didn't really want to look closer at it, but she figured she'd have to. The last guy was poking around the car. He had a T-shirt emblazoned BOMB SQUAD and a heavy-looking helmet, though it was in his hand instead of on his head.

"Lieutenant Webb?" Erin guessed, looking at the guy in the trench coat.

"That's me," he said. "You must be O'Reilly."

"Yeah," she said. "Sorry I'm late. I went to the precinct first."

Webb shrugged. "Glad you could join us. This is Vic Neshenko," he indicated the big man to his right, who grunted and worked a toothpick from one side of his mouth to the other. "And this is Kira Jones," pointing to the woman with the dyed hair, "and our Medical Examiner, Doctor Sarah Levine," finishing with the lab-coated woman. He didn't introduce the bomb-squad guy.

"Good to meet you," Jones said, offering her hand. Erin shook it, noticing deep crimson fingernails through the translucent glove. "That your dog?"

"Yeah, this is Rolf," she said.

"How long have you had him?"

"We've been partnered three years."

"Okay, great," Neshenko said. "And we've worked together for thirty seconds. Can we look at the dead guy so we can go home?"

Erin leaned forward to peer at the corpse at their feet.

"New girl?" Levine said from below.

"Yeah?"

"Move. You're blocking my light."

"Oh. Sorry." Erin stepped to the side, feeling her face flush. She accidentally elbowed the guy in the T-shirt, who'd wandered over.

"Hi," he said, extending his hand. "Skip Taylor, Bomb Squad. I'm not in your unit, of course. And don't worry, the device fully activated. There's no further danger. Say, is your dog trained in EOD?"

"Yeah, he can do explosives detection," she said. "But mostly he does suspect tracking and apprehension."

"That's great," Taylor said. "We've got a K-9 in our unit, but he's training this week, counter-terrorist stuff with Homeland Security and the Feebies. But check out this device, this is some great shit. Took our boy clean out of his shoes. Seriously. You see the shoes over there by the car?"

Erin felt a queasy lump in her stomach. "Yeah, I see," she muttered, turning her attention back to her new commanding officer. "Lieutenant, what'd I miss?"

"Not much," Webb said. "We only got here a few minutes ago. The area's been secured, and Taylor's right. There just seems to be the one bomb. It was enough for this guy, though. The uniform who responded didn't even bother calling for the EMTs."

"I can see why," Neshenko said. "Even dental records aren't gonna do much good. It must've gone off right in his face. His head's practically gone."

"Do we know who he is?" Erin asked.

"We think so," Jones replied. "William O'Connell. His wife called it in, said it was their car."

"It's a nice car," Taylor said. "Expensive Audi, maybe three years old. Well, it was. Now it's scrap metal, with a pretty amazing blast pattern."

No one else seemed too eager to indulge Taylor's enthusiasm for explosive mayhem, but Erin figured there had to be some useful information there. "What's amazing about it?"

"Okay, so the device was under the dash and the driver's seat. It's a two-stage blast, which is unusual by itself," he said. "I'm thinking the initial charge was wired to the ignition and went off right under the steering wheel. That set off the secondary, which was a sizable chunk of what I'm guessing was nitro. But what's weird is, he wasn't sitting in the driver's seat when he got blown away."

"How can you tell?" she asked.

"He's over here," the bomb tech explained. "If the charge had gone off under his ass, it would've blown him straight through the roof of the car and he'd have painted the ceiling."

"Nice," Jones muttered.

"Instead, he got tossed this way. That tells me the device went off when he was standing or maybe bending over. I'm guessing he saw something under the dash, maybe spotted some loose wires or even the device itself, and it went off while he was bent over."

"There's some tools over here," Neshenko said, pointing to the garage floor. "I've got a socket wrench, a screwdriver, and what looks like part of a wire cutter, but it's blown to pieces."

"Jesus," Webb said quietly. "You think he found the bomb and tried to defuse it himself?"

"It's possible," Taylor said. "Stupid of him, but possible. Real civvie move."

"Skip, were you in the service?" Erin asked suddenly. The way he talked, the way he carried himself, and his haircut, all reminded her of Paulson, the former Army Ranger she'd worked with back in Queens.

"EOD, two tours in the sandbox," he said. "Came back with all my parts." He held up a hand and wiggled his fingers.

"What kind of idiot finds a bomb in his car and tries to take it apart instead of calling us?" Webb wondered aloud, returning their attention to the shattered body on the concrete.

"The kind who doesn't want cops around, maybe," Neshenko said, kneeling beside Levine, who was still engrossed in studying the corpse. The big detective flipped back the dead man's suit coat to reveal a shoulder holster, a pistol still strapped in it.

"Damn," Jones said. "He was packing."

"Didn't do him any good," Levine said. "Death was instantaneous. COD was blast trauma and shrapnel that penetrated his face, chest, and neck. The right arm has been amputated just below the shoulder and separated from the torso, coming to rest approximately ten meters away from the principal remains. The left hand has been partially amputated, with the second, third, and fifth fingers missing, but once we analyze the blast pattern a little better, we have a good chance of finding..."

"We get the idea," Webb said. "So he was pretty close to the bomb when it went off?"

"He had his hands practically on it," she confirmed.

"She's right," Taylor said. "I saw some wounds like those in Iraq. There was this one kid, he was screwing around with a landmine..." His voice trailed off and his smile faded.

"Okay," Webb said. "So he had a sidearm and was doing something with the bomb, either trying to figure out what it was or trying to defuse it. Sounds like he might have military experience. What else have we got on him?"

"There's a wallet in his hip pocket," Levine said. "It was shielded from the blast by his body, so appears undamaged.

There's a rolled-up necktie in his left front pocket and keys in his right front."

"Car keys?" Erin asked.

"Car, house, safe-deposit box," Levine said.

"Well, that proves he didn't set it off by starting the engine," Erin said. "They'd still be in the ignition otherwise."

"Seat belt wasn't fastened either," Taylor said. "Not that that proves anything. If he was dumb enough to monkey with a homemade nitro bomb, he probably wasn't smart enough to buckle up."

"What else have we got from the car?" Webb asked.

"Driver's side door over there," Neshenko said, pointing with his thumb. The door had been blasted away from the car at an angle, leaving a streak of black paint on the garage wall before coming to rest in a twisted heap.

"Yeah, I think the door was open when the bomb went off," Taylor said. "If it was only secured by the hinges, it would've angled forward like that. If it'd been closed, it would've gone in more of a straight line."

"So our victim was leaning over the seat with the door open, standing about where his shoes still are," Webb said.

"Just like car crashes," Erin said, her Patrol experience still fresh in her mind. "You can usually judge point of impact when a pedestrian gets run down by where you find the shoes."

"That's right," Webb said. "Okay, we're getting a picture."

"Trunk's open," Neshenko reported. He was prowling around the edges of the crime scene like a restless junkyard dog. "I got a toolbox, open lid, a triple-A kit, and a spare tire."

"All right," Webb said. "So you're all telling me this guy comes down to the garage, is all set to get into his car, and what? Sees a bomb wired to his ignition switch. For some reason he doesn't call the cops and decides to take care of it himself. Probably because he's a moron. He takes off his tie, stows it in his pants pocket, pops the trunk, opens his toolbox, gets out his tools and tries to take the bomb apart. He screws the pooch, the bomb blows up in his face, and here we are. And there he is."

Erin looked around at the others. All of them were nodding.

"So why doesn't he call the cops?" Erin said. "Is this guy on the FBI Top Ten? There's nothing illegal in the trunk. Has he got diamonds in the door panels? Cocaine in the glove compartment?"

"We'll go over the car," Taylor said. "I need to confirm the explosive. I'm only guessing it was nitro. I'll know more when I run the lab tests. If there's anything else in there, we'll find it. We're taking the entire vehicle to the department lot."

"We need to talk to the wife," Jones said.

"Where is she?" Erin asked.

"Upstairs, in their apartment," Webb said. "We've got uniforms with her."

"And she's a real piece of work," Neshenko said.

"What do you mean?" she asked.

"You'll see."

Chapter 2

"Who's taking the lead on the interview?" Erin asked as they rode the elevator to the fourth floor. Neshenko, Taylor, and Levine had remained in the basement, cataloging evidence.

"I am," Webb replied. "But I want you and Jones handy."

"For the woman's touch, you mean?" Jones asked with a wry twist of her mouth.

"Something like that," he said. "And in case you think of something I don't. Have you done many interviews with family members of victims, O'Reilly?"

"Yeah," she said. "Usually car crashes, not homicides." Erin paused. "Sir, is the wife a suspect?"

He raised an eyebrow. "Let's call her a 'person of interest' for the moment."

The elevator came to a halt, interrupting the conversation. The detectives walked to number 415. Webb knocked. A uniformed cop answered and nodded to the lieutenant. They went inside.

Erin's first sense of the place was of clutter. It was a two-bedroom apartment, spacious by Manhattan standards, but it was packed full of furniture and artwork. Some of it might have been good, all of it looked expensive, but there was no pattern to the presentation, so the effect was like a high-class estate sale. She half-expected to see price tags on everything.

"She's in her bedroom," the uniformed officer said, pointing with his thumb.

"*Her* bedroom, or *their* bedroom?" Jones asked.

"Hers, I'd say," the cop said in a low voice. "His is next door."

Webb nodded and motioned the others to follow him.

Stepping through the bedroom door, Erin paused and blinked. The change from the rest of the apartment was startling. The only furniture was a small twin bed, a dresser, and a night table. The rest of the space had been converted into a greenhouse. There was a bank of sun lamps, a clear plastic curtain running across the middle of the room, and the strong smell of roses. She saw rose bushes covered with brilliant blossoms, ranging from pale pastel to deep scarlet.

Another uniformed policeman stood against the wall. A tall, slender woman was inside the greenhouse, bending over one of the plants. She took no notice whatsoever of the new arrivals.

Webb beckoned Erin and Jones. "Mrs. O'Connell?" he called softly.

The woman turned. She had a face that was just a little too angular to be called beautiful. She seemed to be made of sharp ridges and hard lines. She stared at them with an expression of cool, polite interest.

"Yes, I am Cynthia O'Connell," she said. "And who might you be?"

"Lieutenant Webb, NYPD," he answered. "These are Detectives Jones and O'Reilly. Ma'am, I'm very sorry for your loss, and sorry to have to do this, but I need to ask you a few questions."

"I would much prefer you to be prompt than sorry,

Lieutenant," she said. "I have been waiting for you. I would appreciate it if this could be taken care of prior to ten o' clock."

Erin was about to ask why the time was important, but Jones caught her eye and gave a slight shake of her head. Instead of speaking up, she waited and watched, trying to learn. Webb's voice was calm and quiet, if a little flat. Cynthia's manner was matter-of-fact to the point of being cold. Her self-control was amazing, considering her husband had been blown to pieces only a few minutes before. Erin had never seen someone react to any violent death with so little emotion, much less that of a spouse.

The woman's eye fell on Rolf. Her lip curled in distaste. "What is that... *animal* doing?"

Erin glanced at her partner. The Shepherd was, at that moment, doing absolutely nothing. He was on duty, which meant he was standing still, paying close attention to her.

"He's my K-9," Erin said. "He won't do anything I don't tell him to."

"I will hold you responsible for any damage it causes."

"Ma'am, in your own words, can you tell me what happened?" Webb asked, trying to turn the conversation onto its intended course.

"Certainly," Cynthia said, giving no further notice to the dog. "William left the apartment at approximately seven o' clock. A short while later, I felt a violent shock that shook the building. A few minutes after that, Miss Harland knocked on my door."

"Excuse me, ma'am," Webb said. "Who is Miss Harland?"

"A neighbor," Cynthia said. "She is a fellow aficionado of horticulture."

A what of the which? Erin very nearly said out loud. It must have showed on her face.

The woman rolled her eyes ever so slightly. "To put it in

layman's terms, she shares my interest in flowering plants."

"Thank you," Webb said, ignoring the contempt in her voice. "Go on, please."

"She told me that my car had exploded, and that William was dead. She was quite distraught. I went to the garage and confirmed what had occurred. A number of bystanders were present, but none were engaged in any constructive activity. I returned to my apartment and telephoned the police department, whereupon I awaited your arrival."

"When exactly did the explosion occur?" Webb asked.

"I really couldn't tell you, Lieutenant," she said. "I was fully engaged in my preparations for my exhibition. One loses one's sense of time when engaged in one's passions."

"Why did you stay inside when the blast happened?" Erin asked, jumping into the conversation.

Cynthia made an elegant, deliberate motion that suggested a shrug. "It did not appear to concern me. I thought perhaps a gas main had burst, or an automobile accident had occurred. No fire alarms followed, no panic in the hallways, no aroma of combustion."

"If a car bomb went off in my basement, I think I'd recognize it as an explosion," Erin said.

"Perhaps your upbringing was more conducive to familiarizing you with such occurrences than was my own," Cynthia said, her way of elongating words sounding almost British. "Your speech betrays, shall I say, plebeian origins?"

Erin, very aware of her working-class Queens accent, clamped her mouth shut and quietly fumed.

"Ms. O'Connell, can you think of any reason anyone would want to hurt your husband?" Jones asked

"Would you prefer my answers in order of probability, or shall I alphabetize them?" Cynthia replied. Then she gave a theatrical sigh. "William was a man quite skilled at attracting troubles. He was a failure in every entrepreneurial adventure upon which he embarked. You have seen our parlor, much reduced from our former circumstances. He squandered my savings and inheritance, and in the end, he found that the pastime he most enjoyed was the one furthest beyond his intellectual capacity."

"What was that?" Webb asked.

"Please, Lieutenant, my garden club meets at ten, I really must make my preparations and be on my way," Cynthia said. "I can hardly drive myself there now, can I? I shall have to summon a cab. If we might continue this interview at a more opportune moment, perhaps after a few hours' interlude?"

Webb's eyebrows drew together. Erin, having seen that look on men about to get into bar fights, could see that he wasn't as calm as he appeared. "This is a homicide investigation, Mrs. O'Connell," he began.

Erin didn't stop to think. It felt like the right play to make, so she made it. "What do you need to do to get ready for the garden club?" she asked, putting a bright, interested smile on her face.

"I shall be exhibiting my damask roses," Cynthia said. "They have just begun to bloom, and I shall bring several of the blossoms. I must cut them and place them in water."

"May I have a closer look?" Erin said, pointing to the flowers. "They're lovely."

Cynthia, for the first time in the interview, looked genuinely pleased. "Oh, yes," she said. "Very well. You may come in while I cut them. But you mustn't touch anything. And your animal must remain on the far side of the curtain."

"Certainly, ma'am. Rolf, *sitz*," Erin said, using the German commands with which the Bavarian-born Shepherd had been trained. "*Bleib.*"

Rolf obediently sat and stayed, head high, ears perked,

awaiting further orders.

Once in her greenhouse, Cynthia changed. The hard lines on her face softened as she bent over her plants. She seemed almost unaware of Erin's presence.

Erin saw that the roses were indeed beautiful. They were lovingly tended, with full, lush blooms. A heavenly smell filled the air.

"This is a special place for you, isn't it?" she asked quietly. "Away from your husband."

"Precisely," Cynthia said, staring at a pale pink blossom, brushing its petals with her fingertips. "This was one thing William could never take from me. We once inhabited a larger residence, you know."

Erin had already guessed as much, from the cluttered state of the apartment. It had the look of a home that had been downsized. "How did he lose the money?" she asked gently.

"Gambling, naturally," Cynthia replied, still not looking at Erin. "I suppose only real-estate speculation could lose money more swiftly. Unfortunately, he bled our funds away so rapidly that I was only able to protect some of my assets. I am certain he owes more than he ever told me. It is possible his insurance policy will cover his legitimate debts, but I live with the knowledge that unsavory characters may emerge to demand restitution."

Erin blinked. "Are you saying he owed money to mob guys? Organized crime?"

"It would not surprise me in the slightest," the recent widow said with her unshakable coolness.

"Are you sorry he's been killed?" Erin asked.

Now Cynthia did stop attending to her roses, turning her attention back to Erin. "It will cause me considerable legal and financial difficulties," she said calmly. "But so would a divorce. On the whole, William's passing has done me a favor. Nothing in his life so became him as his taking leave of it."

The phrase tugged at a high school memory. "Hamlet?" Erin guessed.

"Macbeth," Cynthia corrected. "But at least you correctly identified the playwright. Perhaps your formative years were not wholly wasted." She turned back to the rosebush, measured the stem with her hand, and expertly snipped off one of the largest blooms. She dropped it at once into a glass of water, which Erin saw had a plastic bag lining it. The woman cinched the bag tight around the stem with a rubber band. "Now, I really must be going."

"I just have one more question, ma'am," Erin said. "Can you tell me who your husband's bookie was?"

Cynthia shook her head. "I am terribly sorry, detective, I cannot." She paused. "There is a safe in his room. I believe he kept his gambling receipts there."

"Do you have the combination?"

"No," the woman said. "But for all I care, you can cut the door off."

Webb didn't want to let Cynthia go, but he wasn't prepared to arrest her yet, either. He compromised by telling her not to leave town and getting her permission to remain in the apartment and search the premises, including opening William's safe. Accordingly, once Cynthia signed her permission, Jones called a locksmith.

"What do you think, O'Reilly?" Webb asked, once Cynthia had gone.

Erin shook her head. "I can see why you'd like her for the bombing, but I don't think it's her."

"Why not?"

"She hated him, that's obvious," she said. "But building a bomb? That'd be way too working-class. She's sees herself as high society. Plus, why take out the car? There's got to be plenty of ways she could've killed him that'd be less expensive. Tidier, too. I see her as more of a poisoner."

"So you're thinking the organized crime angle?" Webb asked.

"Yeah," Erin said. "If he owed money to the mob, they'd totally be willing to blow him up."

"Loan sharks don't like to kill their debtors," Jones pointed out. "They're glad to scare 'em, sure, but they want money. Bodies don't pay the bills."

"He was carrying a gun," Webb said. "It looks like he was expecting trouble. Maybe they scared him too much and he decided to take a stand. It could be they figured the wife would be a softer touch."

"Yeah," Erin said. "Except that now there's cops all over the case. They can't possibly have wanted that."

"Let's see what's in the safe," Webb said. "Maybe it'll give us something to go on."

*   *   *

The locksmith was a small, bespectacled man with watery eyes. He examined the safe with the same expert attention Cynthia had given to her flowers. He took off his glasses, wiped them with a handkerchief, and nodded. "Yes, I can open it," he said.

"That's great," Webb said.

Erin expected him to produce a stethoscope and listen to the dial. Instead, the locksmith began setting up a massive industrial drill. Finesse was going to take a backseat to brute force.

"You may want to wait outside," he said, putting on headphones to insulate himself from the noise. Then the high-pitched whine of the diamond-tipped drill permeated the apartment. It only took a few minutes, but as he was finishing drilling out the lock, Neshenko joined them in the living room.

"The bomb squad's still packing up the pieces," he reported. "You get anything from the wife?"

"Yeah," Erin said. "She hated his guts, he owed money to gamblers, and he saved her having to file for divorce when he exploded."

"Nice," Neshenko said.

"Hey, if they were nice guys, who'd want to murder them in the first place?" Jones asked.

The sound of the drill died away. The locksmith appeared in the doorway. "Done!" he announced. The four detectives hurried into William O'Connell's bedroom.

The safe's contents were unimpressive at first glance. There were no stacks of dollar bills, no sacks of bullion, just a sheaf of papers with cryptic notes filling page after page. Webb pulled on his gloves and flipped through them.

"What've we got?" Neshenko asked.

"Gambling sheets," Webb said. "I've seen this kind of shorthand before. This is a record of O'Connell's bets. Most of them seem to be referencing a bookie who goes by Cars."

"Street name?" Erin guessed.

"Probably," Webb said. "Jones, you want to run the alias?"

"Already on it," she said, tapping her phone's screen. "Just a minute."

"How much was he in the hole?" Erin asked.

"Hard to say," Webb said. "At a glance, I'd say sixty or seventy thousand."

"*Thousand?*" Erin exclaimed. "That's more than I make in a year!"

"I've got something," Jones said. "There's a guy who's known to run a sports book out of his bar. It's an Irish pub, the Barley Corner. His name's Morton Carlyle. His file's thin, but he's a known associate of the O'Malleys."

"Irish mob?" Neshenko guessed.

"Yeah," Jones said. "Rough bunch, pretty well established."

"He have a history of blowing people up?" Webb asked.

"Don't know," Jones replied. "His file says he was suspected of blowing up some garbage trucks in the late '90s, but he's never even been arrested. Not this side of the pond at any rate."

"Is he an immigrant?" Erin asked.

"Looks like he came over from Ireland in '94," Jones said.

"Maybe your family knows him," Neshenko said to Erin.

She gave him a look. "My family's been American for a hundred years," she said. "New Yorkers the whole time. How long since your folks came over from Mother Russia? You've got a bit of an accent."

"Enough with the immigrant profiling," Webb said. "I get it, we're a real ethnic crew. I'm from LA, and that's practically a different planet. Jones, I want you to go back to the office. Find out if they've got anything on this Carlyle where he came from. O'Reilly, Neshenko, you're with me. We need to go talk to this Carlyle character. He's involved, one way or another."

"Hey, Lieutenant, just because it's my first day, you don't have to take me to an Irish bar," Erin said.

Webb blinked and stared at her. There was an awkward pause. Then Neshenko slapped her on the shoulder and grinned. "You're all right, O'Reilly," he said.

"You can call me Erin," she said.

"Then call me Vic."

"Okay," Webb said. "We've gone around in a circle and introduced ourselves. Now let's go see what the Irishman can tell us. And remember, no drinking, even if you're Irish and Russian. We're on duty."

"So, an Irish cop and a Russian cop walk into a bar," Vic said. "The bartender looks at them and says, 'What is this? Some kind of joke?'"

Erin laughed. "Say, can one of you give me a ride?" she asked. "I don't have a car from the motor pool yet."

"How'd you get here?" Webb asked.

"I took a cab," she admitted.

"A Yellow Cab delivering a detective to a crime scene," Vic said. He shrugged. "Goddamn New York City. They let you take your dog?"

"He's a working animal. The first couple passed me by, but the third guy stopped. I tipped him an extra five."

Vic shrugged. "Everyone's got a price."

"It'll be a bit of a squeeze," Webb said. "Neshenko rode with me, so we're only taking the one car."

"I've got shotgun," Vic said immediately.

"Rolf and I will be fine in back," Erin said.

Chapter 3

"So," Erin said as Webb's unmarked Crown Victoria rolled toward their destination, "how long have you guys been on this unit?"

"It's brand new," Webb said. "Expansion of Major Crimes. The Captain brought me on first, six weeks back. The others have been here about a month."

"Where'd you come from?" she asked.

"Los Angeles," Webb said. "I already told you that."

"No, I mean, what was your prior posting?"

"Homicide," he said. "I moved from the LAPD eight years back." He held up a finger. "And I've heard all the LA jokes already, so don't go there."

"How about you, Vic?" she asked.

"ESU," he said. "Tactical unit."

"How do you go from kicking in doors with Emergency Services to working major cases?"

"Same way you got out of Patrol Division," he shot back.

"I went over the head of the Detective Bureau and almost got fired," she said, then wished she could take the words back. She saw Webb's eyebrows in the rearview mirror. They were trying to climb right off his face. "Captain Holliday liked my initiative," she said, more defensively than she'd meant to. "And I did solve the case."

"Yeah, that art thing down in Queens," Neshenko said. "I heard about that."

"So, did Holliday recruit you, too?" she asked.

"Not exactly," the big Russian said. "My commander said it'd be good experience for me."

In Erin's experience, if an officer wasn't specifically requested for a unit, then that officer was probably being transferred because he, or she, was a bit of a problem child. Transfers were a great way for a division to shed dead weight or to get rid of a misfit. What would a guy have to do to get kicked off an ESU team? Erin looked at Vic's rough profile. No doubt about it, he looked like a police brutality suit waiting to happen. But who knew? Maybe he was a marshmallow underneath.

Then again, maybe under the layer of thuggery was just a thug.

* * *

It was just after eleven when the three detectives and one dog walked through the door of the Barley Corner; a little too early for the lunchtime crowd. It was an old brownstone building, with rounded window arches lined with green and gold stained glass.

Erin took in the interior. The Corner was better lit than most pubs she'd been in, so her eyes adjusted quickly. The pub's main room was furnished in dark, worn wood. The woodwork was well cared-for and lovingly polished. The bar was an elbow shape, with the usual assortment of bottles of exotic liquor behind it. There were tables and booths, most of them currently unoccupied, and three large flat-screen TVs showing sporting events.

Erin's policewoman's eye caught the relevant people in the place right away. The bartender, a twentysomething with red hair and a pleasant smile, looked like a civilian. So did the waitress, a pretty young woman sporting a long ponytail and a skirt and blouse high and low enough to attract attention. But the two guys at the corner table with buzz-cut hair and athletic physiques needed watching. She'd have bet a week's salary they were carrying guns and knew exactly how to use them. They were hired muscle, probably ex-military. The other people were customers, big blue-collar guys for the most part. And then there was the man sitting at the bar.

She knew who he had to be right away, even though she didn't have a photo to work from. Everything about him, from his carefully-combed silver hair to his perfectly shined shoes, spoke of control. This was *his* place, and he was completely at home in it. He was dressed conservatively in a dark charcoal sport coat and slacks. He was good-looking in a classic Hollywood way, a little like Richard Gere. His eyes were bright, piercing blue.

He watched them approach, focusing his attention on Erin. His gaze traveled up and down her with nonchalant appreciation. Erin had been leered at by countless street punks, but something in the way Morton Carlyle looked at her made her self-conscious. As a trained dog handler, she knew an alpha male when she saw one. And there was something else. Erin could have sworn he recognized her, though she couldn't recall ever setting eyes on him before.

"Mr. Carlyle?" Webb asked.

"And who would be wanting to know?" he replied, his voice holding the unmistakable brogue of Northern Ireland.

"I'm Lieutenant Webb, NYPD," Webb said, flipping open his wallet to show his shield. "This is Detective Neshenko and

Detective O'Reilly. We'd like to ask you some questions."

"O'Reilly, you say?" Carlyle said, glancing at Erin again. "I'm at your disposal, detectives. Would you be wanting anything with which to refresh yourselves?"

"No, thanks," Erin and Webb said simultaneously.

"Well then, if you'll pardon my own indulgence," Carlyle said. He raised a finger. "Danny?"

The bartender was instantly there. "What can I get you?"

Carlyle leaned over and said something in Danny's ear. The younger man nodded.

"Are you certain?" Carlyle said to the others. "It needn't be spirits. Perhaps a glass of soda water? Come now, it's insulting to an Irishman not to drink with him."

"I'll have a Coke," Erin said.

"Nothing for me," Vic said.

Webb sighed. "Mineral water."

Danny returned. He slid the requested drinks to the police, then put a glass of Guinness on the bar in front of Carlyle. He placed a shot glass on the bar, half-filled with Bailey's Irish Cream. He topped up the shot glass with whiskey from a bottle marked Glen D, an expensive-looking label. Finally, the bartender gingerly lifted the shot glass over the glass of stout and dropped it in.

"Cheers, ma'am, gentlemen," Carlyle said, lifting the glass. He tossed back its contents in a single long drink. That was the way to take the beverage, before the cream had a chance to curdle. Erin took a more measured swallow of her Coke, trying to keep a straight face. She knew what the drink was called, and it was the single cockiest thing Carlyle could have drunk in front of them. He was taunting them without even saying anything.

Carlyle let out his breath slowly. "Well," he said. "Now that we've dispensed with the rituals, what can I do for New York's very finest?"

To Erin's surprise, Webb looked at her and made a slight gesture with his hand for her to talk. A little flustered, very conscious of Carlyle's attention, she started in with the interview.

"Mr. Carlyle, what is your relationship with William O'Connell?"

The Irishman leaned back against the bar, taking his time answering. "There's more than one lad in this city who answers to that name, Miss O'Reilly," he said finally. "To which might you be referring?"

Erin didn't like being baited. "I'm talking about the one who owed you over sixty grand," she said bluntly.

"Miss O'Reilly," Carlyle said. "While the Corner does allow frequent patrons to run a continuous tab, I'm quite certain we've no customers with such a high debt incurred. That would pay for a considerable number of drinks."

"I'm talking about a gambling debt," she said.

"I'm greatly afraid you might be thinking of me as a man engaged in some manner of illegal activity," he replied. "I assure you, this is a reputable establishment. Though surely there's a certain amount of friendly wagering on sporting events, as goes on in any such place."

Erin tried to think how to chip away at the man's polished exterior. He knew why they were there, and what was more, he wanted them to know that he knew. The only reason to play coy with him was that he was wanting to play it that way himself. Webb and Vic were being no help at all; Vic was actually a short distance down the bar, talking to the bartender, while Webb was watching Erin and Carlyle's conversation in silence.

"Do you know much about explosive devices, sir?" she asked, changing tacks with deliberate suddenness, trying to get a reaction.

It didn't work. He raised an eyebrow fractionally, but that was it. "I know they're dangerous, Miss O'Reilly, and good things to steer well clear of."

"Specifically, what do you know about car bombs?" she pressed.

"If you're referring to prior history, I've nothing to say on the matter," Carlyle said. "And if you're referring to anything that may have happened to dear William, I assure you, I had nothing whatever to do with it."

Erin blinked, caught momentarily at a loss for words.

"When things happen in my neighborhood, Miss O'Reilly," he said with a smile, "you should know information finds its way to my ears."

"Okay," Erin said, deciding to bite. "If you're a guy who hears things, tell me what you've heard. Why would someone blow up O'Connell?"

"Miss O'Reilly," Carlyle said, still smiling, "why do you think anyone wanted to kill him?"

"If they didn't, they did a good job of faking it," Erin said. "He's one of the deadest guys I've ever seen."

"And how did you find him at the scene?" he asked.

Webb broke into the conversation. "Mr. Carlyle, we're asking the questions here," he said brusquely. "For obvious reasons, we can't discuss the details of an ongoing investigation. Now, where were you this morning between five and seven thirty?"

"I was upstairs, asleep," Carlyle said. "My place of residence is directly above this public house."

"Can anyone vouch for you?" Erin asked.

He looked her straight in the eye. "I'd no overnight company, Miss O'Reilly," he said.

She felt her face flush slightly. That hadn't been what she'd meant, and he damn well knew it. He was still playing games.

"Did anyone see you coming or going?"

"Aye," he said. "But that proves nothing. After all, one of the joys of an explosive is that one needn't be present when it goes off. Like poison, it works whether the perpetrator is present or not, on whomever happens to get in its way."

"Just so we're clear," Webb said. "You're saying you didn't kill O'Connell, and you don't know who did."

"That's correct, Leftenant," Carlyle said, using the British Isles pronunciation of Webb's rank. "But I wish you the best of luck in your inquiries." He looked at Erin again. "And I do hope you will tell me if I can be of any further service to you."

"That'll be all for now, Mr. Carlyle," Webb said. "Thank you for your time." He turned to Vic. "Time to go, Detective."

Erin started for the door after the others. Then she paused. "Mr. Carlyle, there's just one more thing."

"Certainly," he said.

"I just want to introduce you to my partner," she said. "Rolf, *such*," she ordered, giving the command for him to search and pointing to the publican.

Rolf, ears stiff and alert, approached Carlyle with none of the tail-wagging friendliness of a normal dog. He was on the job, sniffing carefully at the man. Carlyle watched the animal with polite curiosity.

The German Shepherd finished his search and turned to Erin, tail waving uncertainly. He hadn't alerted to anything, which meant Carlyle didn't have any explosive residue that Rolf could smell.

"And what's this lad's name?" Carlyle asked.

"Rolf," Erin said.

"Fine name. Is he a European import as well?"

"Bavarian," she said. "Okay, we're done here." She turned to go once more.

"Miss O'Reilly?" Carlyle's voice followed her.

She turned in the doorway.

"Tell your father an old friend said hello."

Chapter 4

"Sir, with all due respect, what the hell just happened?" Erin burst out.

Webb raised an eyebrow at her. They were standing on the sidewalk a short distance from the Barley Corner. Passersby shot curious looks at them, but she didn't care.

"Got a problem, Erin?" Vic asked. He was smiling a little, as if he got the joke, which didn't help her state of mind at all.

"Is this some kind of hazing thing?" she demanded. "Sir, you threw me in there with no prep, no leverage, and let me just bounce off that guy. He's a serious mobster, and it's my first day on the damn job!"

"You know him?" Webb asked.

"No!"

The Lieutenant raised a hand. "I just thought, with the last thing he said when you left..."

"I don't know what that was about. Maybe he saw my picture in the paper, from the art thing down in Queens. Whatever. Why didn't you talk to him?"

"Because he was talking to you," Webb said.

"Huh?"

Webb shrugged. "Field interrogations and interviews aren't an exact science. With the real hardasses, the toughest thing to do is break through the silence. Whatever gets them talking, you go with that. He was talking to you, so you were the best one to talk to him."

Erin could see his point, when he put it that way. "God, he's a creep," she said. But she didn't mean it. What was unnerving about Carlyle was his confidence and his easy manner, even under police scrutiny. There was something oddly charming about him. She'd been right with her initial assessment. He was an alpha in the rough and tumble pack of the underworld. It made him compelling, but also very dangerous.

"So what do you think, O'Reilly?" Webb asked. "Did he do it?"

"I hope so," Vic muttered.

"Maybe," Erin said. "He's absolutely capable of it. And did you see his drink? Bomb shot of whiskey and Irish Cream into Guinness?"

"Irish Car Bomb," Vic said, getting it. "He's a smug son of a bitch, all right."

"He's messing with us," Erin said. "Which means either he's just having fun jerking us around, or he really did do it and he's sure we can't prove it. But it tells us one thing about him for sure."

"What's that?" Webb asked.

"He knew about the hit on O'Connell before we got there," Erin said. "He knew why we were at his bar. He was *waiting* for us. So he has to have some other information source, if he's not the guy."

"Let's get back to the precinct and see how Jones's research is going," Webb said. "Maybe she can give us the skinny on Mr. Carlyle."

*　　*　　*

As they entered the precinct, Vic put his hands on his hips. "What the hell?" he demanded.

"What's the problem?" Webb asked.

"What's all this shit doing on my desk?"

Erin followed his look and grimaced. She'd put her gear down on the emptiest desk, assuming it was the vacant one. Apparently she'd been wrong.

"That's mine," she said. "Sorry about that." She hurried to clear her belongings away. "Where am I?"

"That one," Vic said, pointing to a desk that had been doing duty as a receptacle for empty pizza boxes and Chinese takeout containers. Erin piled up the trash and crammed it into a garbage can, then came back to join the others.

Jones was busy at her computer. She pointed to a pile of fresh-printed pages on her desk. "This is quite a guy you've got," she said.

"How so?" Webb asked, picking up the papers and flipping through them. Erin saw that they were mostly news printouts from English and Irish papers and websites.

Jones pushed her chair back and ran a hand through her blue-dyed hair. "He's a freaking terrorist, for starters."

"You're kidding," Erin said, fighting the urge to grab the papers out of her Lieutenant's hands.

"Morton David Carlyle," Jones recited, consulting her notepad. "Born February 23, 1964, Belfast, Ireland. Parents: Maureen and Daniel Carlyle. One brother, Norbert, two years younger. Went to Catholic school, was obviously very bright— high grades, especially in chemistry, some academic prizes—but didn't graduate."

"Why not?" Erin asked.

"The Troubles really flared up in the mid-'70s," Jones

explained. "He dropped out of school to join the IRA after his dad was killed."

"Nice," Vic said.

"What I've got of his IRA activities comes mostly from the British side," she continued. "They think he worked with some of the IRA's best bomb-makers, learned everything they knew. He may have been involved in the Mountbatten assassination in '79."

"He'd have only been fifteen," Erin said, doing the math.

"Yeah, a real child prodigy," Jones said. "He's suspected of making bombs that were used in a dozen separate attacks through the '80s. He was arrested and interrogated three times, but they could never make a charge stick."

"So what's he doing over here?" Vic asked.

"He settled down in the early '90s," Jones said. "He married Rose McCann in 1991. She died just two years later, age twenty-one. I found the wedding announcement and the obit in the Belfast Telegraph."

"How'd she die?" Erin asked.

"Paper didn't say," Jones said. "Carlyle left Ireland a couple months later and wound up here. He dropped off the radar for a while, then showed up in some police investigations. I'll get to those in a second. Looks like he fell in with the Irish mob. They'd have found a use for an IRA veteran who knew his way around bombs."

"Is he a suspect in any bombings on this side of the ocean?" Webb asked.

"Nothing definite," Jones said. "But he was a person of interest in a couple unsolved bombings be connected to the O'Malleys, some stuff with garbage trucks in Queens in the late '90s. Other than that, he's clean. Never been charged, never even arrested over here. The only reason we have his prints on file is from his immigration papers."

"I want some more legwork on this," Webb said. "We need to know who Carlyle's connected to, and why he'd want O'Connell dead. I don't buy the gambling debt idea. Jones is right; if O'Connell owed Carlyle sixty grand, that's sixty thousand reasons for O'Connell to kill Carlyle, not the other way round. But that doesn't mean Carlyle's not our guy. If they were connected through the O'Malleys, there could be any number of reasons to whack him. Maybe they just didn't like each other."

"O'Connell was carrying," Erin said. "He could've been an enforcer for the mob."

"Maybe so," Webb agreed. "That's a good angle to work, too. I think we need to take a good, close look at the Irish mob."

Vic stared at Erin. "You okay with this?" he asked. "Going against your own people?"

"My dad was a cop," Erin snapped. "And so am I. You're more my people than they are." She paused. "Well, Webb and Jones are my people. I'm not sure about you."

Vic grinned. "Stop it, Erin. I may start to like you."

"Okay, everyone, time to get to work," Webb said. "O'Reilly, you look up our victim's mob connections. Get off your ass and knock on some doors. Give a call to Vice; they may have something on the gambling angle, or anything else he may have been into. Neshenko, look up O'Malley associates who might be involved. Jones, keep doing what you've been doing. Find me something more on Carlyle. I'll talk with the bomb squad about the explosive; see if we're making any progress on physical evidence." He clapped his hands. "Let's do this."

*   *   *

Erin didn't yet know the layout of Precinct 8, so it took her a while to find her way to Vice. The Vice department was small, shoved into a room that looked like it might once have been a maintenance closet. A sour-faced man with a drooping left eyelid looked up at her when she cautiously knocked. He didn't say anything, and completely ignored Rolf. Rolf returned the favor.

"Excuse me," she said. "I'm looking for Vice."

"Isn't everyone?" he deadpanned.

Erin nodded good-naturedly. "I'm Erin O'Reilly. Transfer from One-Sixteen down in Queens."

"Tad Brown, Vice," he said with a strong Brooklyn accent. "Sergeant Brown, but that don't mean much when I've got just two officers reporting to me. What unit you in?"

"Major Crimes."

He pursed his lips in a soundless whistle, pretending to be impressed. "Well, well, you married into royalty. What can I do for the princess?"

Oh God, Erin thought. On her first day, that was just the sort of nickname that might stick. "None of that, Sarge," she said, deciding to play it as close to the street as she could and making no effort to mask her own blue-collar roots. "I'm just another shield on the Job. I need to know about gambling around here."

"What sort of action you looking for?"

"Sports book," she said. "Anything involving the O'Malleys."

Brown's right eyebrow rose. Erin noticed that the muscles on the left side of his face didn't work quite right. A long, ugly scar ran down his face just in front of the ear, probably a relic of some street brawl. "You messing with them? You gotta be careful, O'Reilly. Fresh on the job and you step in something like that, you don't walk away with a nice, rosy smell."

"So you know them," she said. "What can you tell me?"

"They're bad news," Brown said. "They're into all kinds of shit. Drugs, hookers, construction rackets, you name it. When Giuliani took down the big Italian mobs in the '90s, guys like them moved in and scooped up the leftovers. The boss is Evan O'Malley. A real old-school S.O.B. Never does anything dirty himself, but he's one of the major players in south Manhattan, along with a chunk of Queens and Brooklyn. He's got his fingers in everything south of the East Village."

"How about Morton Carlyle?" Erin asked.

Brown looked blank for a second. Then he nodded. "Oh, you mean Cars. No one calls him Morton. I mean, how can you take a gangster seriously, he's got a name like that?"

"Cars, then," she said. "What's he into? Who's he run with?"

Brown sighed. "I don't got much of a file on him," he said. "He does sports book, like you said, but he's not on the muscle side of the family, and he don't do the protection rackets. He's kind of a gentleman, they say. He don't touch drugs or girls. Keeps his nose pretty clean, so we can't pin him down. But he's O'Malley's golden boy, for sure. Guys in the know say he's in line to take over the family one of these days, when the old man steps down or gets popped." A flicker of interest was in the Vice sergeant's eyes. "What's he done?"

"He might've blown up a guy with a car bomb," Erin said. "What do you think?"

"Could be," he said with a shrug. "I dunno. Evan's guys sometimes do that shit, but not lately. Nowadays, you blow up something in New York, you got Homeland Security on your ass, and no one wants that kind of trouble."

"But you've been looking into Carlyle's activities?" she pressed.

Brown shrugged again. "We don't have the manpower to break up gambling rings," he said. "It's not a departmental priority. Right now we're cracking down on streetwalkers, and like I said, he don't touch that kind of thing. I think we got a file here, but it'll be thin." He pivoted in his chair to an actual file cabinet. In this digital age, Erin liked the idea of a physical file.

It made her think of her dad. That thought brought her right back to Carlyle's parting words, wiping the smile off her face. *Tell your father an old friend said hello.* What had he meant by that?

"Here we go," Brown said, pulling out a manila folder. He handed it to Erin. "Everything we got on him is in there. Take a look, but it's gotta stay in this room. I can make copies if you want."

Erin looked through the file. It was as skinny as he'd said. Carlyle's immigration papers from INS were on top. There were some officer reports talking about the Barley Corner as a front for alleged gambling activity, but that seemed to be all Vice had on him. She noted a cross-reference to a file with Alcohol, Tobacco, and Firearms, but since the ATF was federal, she didn't have anything to go on. She pointed to it. "How'd he catch the Feds' attention? Liquor licensing?"

"Don't think so," Brown said, glancing down at it. "I think it was something about gunrunning a few years back, but I don't really remember. The national boys grabbed it up, and that was the last anyone saw of it."

Erin nodded absently, continuing to scan the documents. Carlyle had a list of known associates, but there were a lot of names on it. "I'm going to want a copy of this," she said. "Come to think of it, we'll want the whole file, if you can."

"Sure thing, Detective," he said. "I'll run 'em through the machine." He turned to a copier whose plastic had turned yellow with age. As he began feeding pages through it, he talked over his shoulder. "So whaddaya think of the old Eightball so far?"

"Hard to say. This is my first day."

"Very first, huh? Welcome to the big leagues. You're working for Webb, right?"

"Yeah. Anything I should know?"

"Nah," Brown said. "Nothing much, except he thinks it's

still the Fifties. You can tell from the way he dresses. He's an asshole, of course, but he's a Lieutenant, so that comes with the territory."

"Thanks for the heads-up."

"Don't mention it," Brown said. "I mean it. Don't. We don't like to attract attention here. You stick your neck out, you'll get the Bloodhound sniffing round."

"Bloodhound?" she said. But Brown had said everything he meant to on the subject. He handed over a photocopy of the Vice file on Morton Carlyle.

"Here you go, O'Reilly. Good to meet you," he said. It was clearly a dismissal, so Erin left him to his dismal little office.

Chapter 5

Back in Major Crimes, Erin logged onto the department's database and started pulling information on the O'Malleys. She paid no attention to the time. Jones's knuckles rapping on the edge of her desk startled her out of her technological daze.

"What is it?" Erin said.

"We've been taking lunch at twelve-thirty," Jones said, flicking a thumb at the clock. "There's a Chinese place just down the block. You want to come?"

"Sure," she said. "Rolf could use a walk, too." The Shepherd, who had been lying beside her desk, jumped eagerly to his feet.

"So, you find anything?" Erin asked her new coworker as they went downstairs. "There was something in Carlyle's Vice file referencing an ATF probe."

"Yeah," Jones said. "I found that, too. I actually just got off the phone with the Feds. It sounds like Carlyle was a suspect in a major gun-smuggling investigation, but they lost track of the shipment. Military assault rifles from Europe. Some of the guns got found, but they couldn't trace the sale back to him. I've got a request out to Washington, to see what else they can tell me. This guy's dangerous."

"I'm getting that idea," Erin said. "But Sergeant Brown said he didn't think Carlyle did muscle jobs."

Jones nodded, going out the front door of the precinct and holding it for Erin. "Doesn't mean he didn't make the bomb for somebody else," she said. "He could've had one of his guys plant it."

"Makes sense," Erin agreed. "Hey, I've got a question."

"Yeah?"

"I've been hearing something about not wanting to get the Bloodhound's attention. You know anything about that?" Seeing Jones's strange look, she elaborated. "I just don't want to get on anyone's wrong side. I don't know my way around yet."

"His name's Lieutenant Keane, our Internal Affairs guy," Jones said. "You met him yet?"

"No," Erin said, but she remembered something Holliday had told her at their first meeting. "I think he may have gotten me this job."

Jones didn't look happy at the news. "You be careful around him. I'm not kidding. Watch yourself."

"Okay," Erin said, mystified. "But isn't that IA's job? To keep an eye on us?"

"Yeah," Jones replied. "But he's different. He's the youngest guy to make Lieutenant in the NYPD. He's building a career, and that means making cases. You step out of line in front of him, and he will eat you up and spit out the bones."

"Thanks," Erin said, thinking this was turning out to be one hell of a first day. Apparently the guy who'd recommended her for her position had everyone in the precinct scared to death and their chief bombing suspect was a former terrorist and gunrunner. There'd be no easy learning curve in Major Crimes.

* * *

Erin's afternoon was nothing but dead-ends and pointless speculation. She had one person she could talk to about Carlyle, but she didn't want to do it from work. She had to be alone when she made the call. This wasn't an informant; this was her dad. She was impatient for the day to end, but worried about what would happen once it did.

Carlyle had called Sean O'Reilly an old friend. Was he suggesting her dad had been connected to the Irish mob? That didn't seem possible. He'd always been rock solid, a man who believed in telling the truth, upholding the law, standing his ground. That was part of why he'd never made it past Sergeant. He didn't know how to play politics.

Carlyle was just messing with her, trying to rattle her. And damn it all, he was succeeding. How had he known who she was? He'd recognized her even before Webb had identified her. He must've seen her picture from the art gallery heist. Erin, not for the first time, cursed all reporters.

While she ran out the clock on her shift, she compared notes with Vic. The big Russian shook his head when she asked how it was going.

"There's gotta be a connection," he said. "Irish guy gets blown up, owes money to another Irish guy who just happens to be a former bomb-maker. Coincidence? Bullshit."

"I'm thinking O'Connell probably worked for him, maybe low-level," she suggested. "Maybe he was working off his debt."

Vic nodded. "Could be. If he owed more than he could pay, he might've seen what else he could do for them, so they didn't start breaking his fingers."

"Which gets us where?"

"Nowhere," he sighed. "It just means they knew each other, and we already knew that from the gambling slips. It's tough breaking up mob organizations. No one wants to talk to the cops. It's not like we can ask them about each other. Hell, we can't ask anyone who knows them. No one's going to share anything. They're a lot more scared of each other than they are of us."

They kept looking for connections, but O'Connell wasn't mentioned in Carlyle's slim file. The hands on the clock on the department wall went gradually round and round, until five o'clock came.

Captain Holliday emerged from his office, settling a battered old hat on his head. "Good night, detectives," he said.

"Don't worry," Webb said to Erin. "They only solve the cases in the first hour on TV. You didn't do badly, for your first day."

"Thanks," she said, though it wasn't much of a compliment.

"See you tomorrow," Jones said. Vic grunted noncommittally and stalked out of the office without a word. Erin nodded, lost in her own thoughts, and headed home with Rolf in tow.

*   *   *

The rush hour subway was crowded, but there were definite advantages to having a ninety-pound German Shepherd. Rolf was good at commanding his space. Breathing room automatically opened around them.

By the time they'd made their way back to her apartment in Queens, taken their evening walk, and thrown dinner in the microwave, it was after six. She couldn't put it off any longer. Her parents' dinnertime was seven o'clock, and her dad tended to doze off after eating. She took out her phone, stared at it for a couple minutes to psych herself up, and hit her speed-dial.

"Hello," her mother said. Mary O'Reilly was a stout, good-natured woman, with a voice that made people think of cozy fireplaces and kitchens that smelled like fresh baking.

"Hi, Mom," she said. "It's Erin. Is Dad—"

"Oh, Erin! I'm so glad you called!" Mary interrupted. "How was your first day at your new job?"

Erin had to smile. Her mother was the conversational gatekeeper of the household, and she had to pay the toll if she wanted to get past. She usually didn't mind, but this time, she was too agitated to really appreciate catching up. She gave a brief account of her coworkers and the precinct.

"Here's the thing, Mom," she said in an effort to steer the conversation. "We've already landed a case, and I need to talk to Dad about it. I'm afraid this is a work call."

"Oh, of course, dear," Mary said, sounding a little disappointed. "But you really should call more often. I feel like I don't know what's happening in your life. Are you seeing anyone right now?"

"Not since Luke," Erin said, fighting the urge to roll her eyes. "Mom, this isn't the best time for me to be thinking about relationships."

"If you wait for the perfect time, you'll run out of time," Mary said. "You're not getting any younger, dear, and if you're wanting children—"

"*Mom*," Erin said. "Can we please not talk about that right now? It's not like you're not already a grandma. You've got Anna and Patrick." They were her oldest brother Sean Junior's kids.

"Yes, and they're such wonderful children," Mary said. "Just think how nice it would be. You don't have to choose between career and family, you know. Things aren't the way they were when I was your age…"

To Erin's relief, she heard her father's voice in the background. "Leave the girl alone, Mary," he said. "You know how O'Reillys react to pressure."

"All right," Mary said, sounding a little hurt. "Here's your father, Erin. But you really should call me when you have a little more time. I miss our talks."

"Sure thing, Mom," Erin said. "I love you."

There was a short pause, then Sean O'Reilly's voice came down the line more clearly. "Okay, kiddo, your mom's gone to work on dinner. What's up?"

"Dad, I'm working a case." She took a deep breath. "I met a guy who said to tell you an old friend said hello."

"This guy have a name?"

"Morton Carlyle," she said. "I've heard people call him Cars."

There was such a long silence on the other end of the line that Erin was afraid the call had disconnected. "Dad?"

"I'm here," he sighed. "Cars Carlyle. I haven't heard that name in years."

"Is he?"

"Is he what?"

"An old friend?"

"No!" he said, almost snapping at her. Then he amended, "At least, I don't think so. It's complicated."

Erin felt a cold hollowness in the pit of her stomach. "Dad, what are you talking about?"

"It's not much of a story, and it's almost twenty years old."

"Dad, I need to know about this guy."

"Why?"

"Because he's a person of interest in a car bombing. A man got blown up this morning, and he's involved. The victim owed him a lot of money, gambling debts."

"Hmm," Sean said, and Erin pictured him thoughtfully stroking his mustache. "Well, we did think Cars was behind some garbage-truck bombings back in the '90s. That's how he got his nickname, you know. Because the word on the street was that he knew everything about how to blow up a car."

"Garbage trucks? What was it, vandalism?"

"No," he said. "This was before your time on the force. I

don't know if you remember, but the Mafia used to run the garbage business in all five boroughs. It's funny, people think about the mob's money coming from drugs, prostitution, that sort of thing, but it turns out there's millions of dollars in garbage collection. Do you have any idea how much trash needs to be hauled out of New York every day?"

"Lots," Erin said.

"Tons of the stuff, and the Mafia controlled the whole thing. They monopolized the industry, made a real killing. But they didn't have it all their own way. There was a major undercover operation in the early '90s to break up the garbage cartels. And some competitors tried to break into the business. Down in Queens in '94 and '95, there was an immigrant gang that tried to strong-arm the Italians, beating up their drivers, blowing up their trucks, that sort of thing."

"So Carlyle was working with them," Erin said. "Is that how you met him?"

"Not exactly. Look, kiddo, there's some things here... it's ancient history."

"Not anymore," she said. "I talked to him this morning. He knew stuff about me. I have to have something; I'm going to need to go back there soon, and I need an edge."

Sean paused again. "Okay," he said finally. "The cops were getting ready to move on the garbage organization. This was in '95. It turned out my partner was into something heavy. He was taking money from the Italians."

"Jesus," Erin said. "Which partner was it?" Her thoughts were racing, thinking of the various men her father had worked with over his career. "Oh God, it was Nate, wasn't it." She remembered the small, cheerful guy who'd come to dinner with them more than once. She also remembered that, while she'd been in high school, her dad had suddenly changed partners and Nate had never come to the house again. She'd never found out what had happened to him.

"Good memory," her dad said. "I knew he was into something a little shady, but I wasn't sure how deep it went. And he was my partner. If you go upstairs on your partner, word gets around the precinct, and pretty soon no one trusts you. I knew it wasn't right to keep my mouth shut, but I didn't know the right thing to do. I was still trying to figure it out when Cars came by."

"He came to the house?" Erin exclaimed.

"Yeah. Just the once."

"Did you know who he was?"

"Yeah," he said again. "We'd run into each other on the street a few times. He wasn't like most of the gangsters. He was always well-spoken, a real smart guy, could even be fun to talk to. And he didn't antagonize the police. You'd have thought he was a civilian if you didn't know better, but I knew his rep."

"What'd he want?"

"He had something for me," Sean said. "An envelope."

Erin closed her eyes. "You took *money* from a *gangster*?" The cold feeling in her stomach was back.

"It wasn't money," he said sharply. "It was bank records, photographs, and a copy of a court order. It was a whole Internal Affairs case against my partner, and there was evidence I'd been complicit with him."

"But you weren't," Erin said with more conviction that she felt at that moment.

"No," he said. "But I could've been, as far as they knew. The way IA was working at the time, they'd have burned both of us. At best, I was looking at early retirement, forced out without my pension."

"How'd Carlyle get his hands on all that?"

"He didn't say, and I didn't have the chance to ask. He handed over the envelope and left before I'd opened it. What it was, was a lifeline. I turned over all of it to our IA guy, said it had been an anonymous package left on my doorstep. And I agreed to testify against Nate." Erin heard the pain in her father's voice at the memory of the old betrayal. "I had to turn in my own partner to save myself. And Cars knew I'd do it."

"Why'd he help you?"

"He never said," Sean said. "I think it was just a favor."

In the distance, Erin heard her mother call, "Dinner's ready!"

"A favor?" she repeated.

"Yeah. That's how the mob runs, how it's always run," he said. "It's all about favors. The money's just for the outside world. Once you're inside, what matters is what you've done for everybody else, and what you can still do for them. Carlyle did me a favor, so he'd have me owing him one. And the bastard never called it in."

*   *   *

Erin didn't have an easy time getting to sleep that night. What she wanted was to go straight down to the Barley Corner and have it out with Carlyle. But she couldn't do that. She was a detective, working a case, and she had to be smart. Whatever her family's history with the Irish mobster, she couldn't let that get in the way of solving O'Connell's murder.

Eventually, she got out of bed and went to her couch. She turned on the TV and let herself zone out in front of it, hoping her brain would slow down enough to let her lose consciousness. What she got was a mid-'90s action movie in which the hero was trying to stop a mad bomber from blowing up a bus. She couldn't help smiling at the connection to her investigation. She let herself enjoy the mindlessness of Hollywood cops, then dozed off with the TV still running.

She sat up suddenly, blinking at the screen. The movie was

about halfway done. She'd nearly missed something. The hero had made his way under the bus to the bomb and recognized something about it. It was a personal memento, a calling card the bomber had left. He'd done it on purpose, to lure the good guys into a trap. Erin, mind still a little foggy, rubbed her temples. Why was that important? Real bombers didn't use calling cards. Did they? She didn't know much about bombs. But there was someone she could talk to who did.

She got off the couch, went into the kitchen, and scribbled a note on her Post-It pad. It said, *Talk to Skip.* She slapped it on the fridge where she'd be sure to see it in the morning.

Apparently, her brain had just been waiting for her to have a direction to take. All the stress and confusion of her first day caught up with her. She barely made it to bed before falling fast asleep.

Chapter 6

Erin was up early, wide awake and rested, eager to take on the day. Rolf, sensing her energy, was as ready to get started as she was. She took him on their usual morning run, grabbed a quick shower, and set off for work. She still didn't have a car, so it was the subway again.

Jones was the only one in the office when Erin arrived just before eight. The smell of coffee caught Erin's nose and she made a beeline for the break room to grab a cup. It tasted like shit. Erin walked over to Jones's desk, taking small, cautious sips.

"Hey, O'Reilly," Jones said. "I see you made it back for round two. Vic didn't scare you off?"

"He's not that scary," Erin said.

"He's exactly that scary," Jones replied. "He's too smart for pure tactical work, but too violent for most other jobs in the department."

"That's why he's here, working Major Cases?" Erin asked, leaning a hip against the edge of the desk and taking another sip of coffee. It wasn't growing on her.

"He's got an eye for weakness," Jones said. "He's good at getting suspects to fold. Sometimes all he needs to do is lean over them and scowl. And if things ever get tough, he's an excellent shot, especially with a rifle."

"Does that happen much?"

Jones shrugged. "This unit's new. We haven't done much of anything yet, including swapping bullets with bad guys. I've never fired my piece in the line, if that's what you're wondering."

"Did you work with Vic, or any of the others, before coming here?"

Jones shook her head.

"Then how come you know so much about him?"

"I read his service jacket. And I asked around."

Erin nodded thoughtfully. "Jones? You transferred out of Internal Affairs, didn't you."

Jones laughed quietly. "Okay, I see why they grabbed you. You've got good instincts. Yeah, I used to be IA. But I'm really an okay girl, once you get to know me. I did some work with the gang task force as a liaison, too, so I'm real police."

"Why'd you make the switch from IA?"

"It was all bureaucratic bullshit," Jones said. "I'm good at it, but I wanted to go after real criminals, not guys who were trying to game the system or juke their stats. I wanted to see some action."

"Speaking of action," Erin said, "what's our protocol? If I've got an idea, a direction I want to take things, do I run it past the Lieutenant first, or do I just do it?"

"We're pretty free-form," Jones said. "But we don't want people doubling up on effort. Shoot him a text, or leave a note on his desk, if he's not around, but clear things in person when you have the chance. What's your plan?"

"I want to talk to the bomb squad about the blast."

"Oh, go on down," Jones said. "They're in the basement, level 2. I'll tell the boss where you are when he shows up."

*   *   *

Erin found the right door without any trouble. Some smart-ass had stuck a skull-and-crossbones sign on it with the label WARNING: MINEFIELD, and even strung a few strands of barbed wire just above head height. Under that sign was a more serious one. It said, IF DOOR IS CLOSED, RING BELL. DO NOT OPEN DOOR WITHOUT PERMISSION. She obediently pushed the doorbell and waited.

Skip Taylor opened the door. He had a pair of needle-nose pliers in his hand, an iPod clipped to his belt, earbuds looped around his neck, and a cheerful smile on his face.

"Morning!" he said. "O'Reilly, right? C'mon in!"

"Erin is fine," she said.

"Okay, Erin. Welcome to the blasting pit." He gestured to the room. It was mostly bare concrete, with shelf units lining the walls and a wooden work table. In the middle of the room was a scattering of familiar-looking scrap metal.

"That's from the explosion yesterday," she said.

"Yup," Skip said, looking pleased. "I've been putting the car back together. If you can line up the pieces just right, you can tell where in the car the explosion originated."

"I've got some questions about the bomb," she said. "Rolf! *Komm hier!*"

Her partner had adopted his "alert" posture, sitting bolt upright and staring at a shelf. On hearing his partner's command, he returned obediently to her side.

"Sure thing, Erin," Skip said. "What do you want to know?"

"I know you've already reported the materials," she said. "We have that info upstairs. What I'm looking for is the signature."

He grinned at her. "Been reading up on mad bombers?"

"Actually, I was watching *Speed* on TV last night," she

admitted a little sheepishly.

Skip laughed. "I've seen that one," he said. "Sorry to disappoint, but this device didn't have a wristwatch stuck to it."

"What can you tell me about the bomb-maker?" she asked. "What's his style?"

"He doesn't have one."

Erin's face fell. "Oh."

"Hey, that's not all bad," Skip said. "It tells us something important."

"Yeah?" She looked at him, trying to gauge whether he was pulling her leg. "What?"

"This one wasn't set by a pro."

"How can you tell?"

"I dismantled a couple hundred IEDs over in Iraq," he said. "Just about everything you can rig to explode. Grenades, artillery shells, land mines, plastic explosive, sticks of dynamite, you name it. After a while, you get a feel for the craftsmanship. The expert bomb-builders are artists. You can tell when a guy knows what he's doing. I'm not talking about anti-tampering devices, any of that crap. It's more like, things move smoothly. Everything's where it's supposed to be. The Unabomber was like that. He'd polish the inside of the casings on his bombs. The *inside*. He took that much pride in his work. This guy here? No pride at all. This was amateur hour."

"It worked well enough," Erin said.

"I'm not sure about that."

"O'Connell's dead, isn't he?"

"Well, yeah, but that's not the point," Skip said. "You could take him out with enough C4 to bring down the whole apartment building and he'd be dead, but that wouldn't make it a professional job. This bomb wasn't placed right. There was too much explosive. It was just plain sloppy."

"That doesn't sound like an experienced IRA car bomber to

me," Erin said.

"You talking about Cars Carlyle?" Skip asked.

Erin blinked. "You know him?"

"Only by reputation," he replied. "Hey, if an IRA veteran lives in my neighborhood, I want to know about him. I've never met him face-to-face, but I heard about the garbage-truck bombings."

"Do you think he could've done this bomb?"

"He could've," Skip said. "But I don't think he would. I've studied some of his overseas work, along with the files on the garbage trucks. His *alleged* bombings. His devices aren't fancy, but they work flawlessly. He's always careful to avoid collateral damage. They're precision instruments, shaped charges. Unless he's deliberately hiding his skill, he didn't make this bomb."

Erin nodded, but her thoughts were spinning. Carlyle was their best lead, and he certainly knew more about the case than he should. On the other hand, everything in his manner at their meeting the day before suggested a man who wanted people to know what he was up to. Would a man like that deliberately disguise his style? She needed to dig deeper on him.

"Thanks, Skip," she said. "That's a big help."

"No prob," he said. "Come by anytime. Tell you what, I'll drop you a line the next time we're gonna blow up some ordnance. You can come along, ride out of town and see some fireworks."

"Sounds fun," she said, laying a hand on the door. "Say, Skip?"

"Yeah?"

"Why do they call you that?"

He smiled. "Old joke from my time in EOD," he said. "We had this great big truck we'd drive to bomb-disposal sites. Somebody in my squad named it The Boat, and that got us thinking a boat needed a captain. I was the driver, so they started calling me Skipper, Skip for short. Crazy, really. I was just a corporal."

"What's your real name?"

He shook his head. "I don't think I'm gonna tell you that."

"I could find out."

"Okay, Detective," he said. "Detect. I'm not gonna help you. Everybody needs practice."

Laughing, Erin left the blasting pit and went back upstairs.

*   *   *

She found Vic, Jones, and Webb all clustered around Jones's computer. "Hey, Erin," Jones said. "Come take a look at this."

Erin joined them. She saw a list of numbers and cryptic letters, recognizing it as the gambling slips they'd found in O'Connell's safe. "What's up?" she asked.

"I think I've got an ID on another of the guys our victim owed money to," Jones said. She pointed to a line labeled FERG. "Once we were working the Irish mob angle, I decided to look for possible matches. Here's what I got." She brought up another window.

A mug shot of a tough-looking guy with an impressive Celtic knotwork tattoo on his neck filled the screen. "Franklin Fergus, AKA Frankie Fingers," Jones said. "Small-time hood. A few busts for unlicensed gambling, paid some fines, with a couple assault raps. Did fifteen months upstate back in '09 for breaking all the fingers on both a guy's hands."

"Hence the nickname," Webb muttered.

"What's his connection to the O'Malleys?" Erin asked.

"Hard to say," Jones said. "He's probably more competitor than collaborator to Carlyle. And he's definitely more of an enforcer."

"No, Carlyle's smoother than that," Erin said. She couldn't

picture him breaking a man's fingers. "How much was O'Connell in the hole to Frankie for?"

"Nothing," Jones said.

"Nothing?" Vic echoed. "Then what's the big deal?"

"He was in deep until recently," Jones said. "I found some older slips that have him owing fifteen large, but they've all got notes in O'Connell's handwriting indicating they're canceled."

"So he got his debt paid off," Webb said. "You think Fergus waited until he'd gotten his money, then whacked O'Connell?"

"It's possible," Jones said. "I'm just looking at the what. I can't tell the why."

"We definitely need to talk to Fergus," Webb said. "Neshenko, O'Reilly, why don't you go see him? Vice has him listed as doing business at a joint called Bernie's over on 36th."

"Sure thing," Vic said.

"Sir, I need a car," Erin said. "Rolf needs a K-9 modified vehicle, with a remote door so I can deploy him."

"I know," Webb said. "When I heard you'd be joining the squad, I filed the request with the motor pool. I haven't heard back yet. Go down to the garage and see if there's any movement on that. If not, see if you can requisition a marked squad with the right specs. It's not ideal, I know, but it's better than nothing."

"Thanks, sir."

Erin, Vic, and Rolf went to the elevator. "You want to drive, or are you okay with a woman doing it?" she asked him as they descended.

"You go ahead," Vic said. "I took out two parking meters and a stoplight the last time I pulled a guy over."

"Bullshit," said Erin.

"Okay, it wasn't quite that bad," he admitted. "But it's still probably better if you're at the wheel."

Erin knew the speed at which bureaucracies usually moved,

so she was pleasantly surprised to find a black Dodge Charger waiting for her in the garage, complete with K-9 compartment. It wasn't brand-new; she suspected it was a repainted patrol car. When she opened the door, she recognized the smell of strong disinfectant that characterized a well-used police vehicle. People threw up in squad cars, they bled on the upholstery, and they tracked in all sorts of awful things. They were worse than inner-city taxis.

She got Rolf situated while Vic folded himself into the passenger seat. Then she adjusted her seat and mirrors to match her height, several inches shorter than the average NYPD driver. "Okay, here we go," she said, turning the key. Her patrol car in Queens had been a Charger about the same age, and the throaty roar of the engine sounded like an old friend's greeting.

"So," Vic said. "We're gonna brace this guy, see what he knows about O'Connell. Ask him about the debt cancellation, see what he gives up?"

"Yeah," Erin said. "You want to try the good cop/bad cop thing?"

"Sure," he said. "Which do you want to be?"

"You really think you can play good cop?" she said, raising an eyebrow.

"Everyone says that about me," Vic said. "Is it the broken nose?"

"I think maybe it is," she said. "You kinda look like a thug. No offense."

"None taken."

Chapter 7

Bernie's was a seedy bar, in a seedy neighborhood. It was squeezed between a payday loan office and the sort of video store that had a few ordinary movies just inside and a big back room full of the dirty stuff. Erin couldn't help comparing it to the Barley Corner. The Corner was a classy place. Bernie's looked like the sort of place they'd put on a billboard for Alcoholics Anonymous as a warning to drunks that they'd hit rock bottom.

"You want to bring the dog in?" Vic asked.

Erin thought about it. "Not right away," she said. "I don't want to spook Frankie." She left the window down a couple of inches, though the day wasn't too warm.

"Okay," Vic said. He looked the building over. "That's gotta be a front. Nobody's gonna hang out in a place like that unless it's a cover for something else."

She nodded, squared her shoulders, and walked in.

The interior was dark and smelled terrible. She squinted, trying to adjust to the dimness, and saw three muscular guys at the bar, watching a TV that was the only expensive thing in the place. The bartender was a short, fat man with a pockmarked face, a sleazy mustache, and a sour expression.

The three toughs at the bar glanced at the newcomers. "Hey babe," the one on the left said. "I think maybe you're in the wrong place, but if you want, I can make it the right one." He had a shaved head and was wearing a wife-beater that showed off tattooed arms. Erin recognized some of his tats as prison-yard ink.

She sighed. Guys like this were so predictable. They were all posture, especially to a woman. They weren't even trying to impress her; just one another. She ignored him and looked at the other two. One of them was enough like the first that they could've been brothers, down to a matching tattoo of a cobweb on his bicep. That was a common prison tat that meant the wearer had done time. The other guy matched the mug shot she'd seen back at the precinct. Franklin Fergus wasn't very tall, but he was built like a brick, broad-shouldered and strong. He had short, spiky hair and two-day stubble on his chin. He flexed his hands as he looked at her and Vic, cracking his knuckles.

"Franklin Fergus?" she asked, addressing the third guy.

"Say who?" he shot back.

"Frankie Fingers?" Vic translated.

"What about him?" Frankie asked. He stood up, as did his two compatriots. Erin found herself wishing she'd brought Rolf after all. She was getting a really ugly vibe from these three.

"Neshenko and O'Reilly," Vic said. "NYPD."

"Ah, shit," Frankie said. Then he turned and ran for the back door.

"Dammit!" Vic snapped. He lunged after the fleeing man. Erin hesitated an instant, debating going outside for Rolf. But there wasn't time. The two thugs stepped in Vic's way. The room was narrow and the big Russian couldn't get around them.

Vic wasn't much on diplomacy. The men were deliberately obstructing him, so he didn't waste time asking them to move.

He grabbed the guy on the left by the belt with one hand and under the chin with the other and threw him over the bar. The bartender let out a startled yelp and ducked. Glass shattered and the man landed with a crash.

Vic tried to shoulder past the other guy, who was momentarily frozen in shock, as was Erin. Then things happened fast. The guy Vic had thrown came up roaring, scalp streaming blood from a shallow gash. The other goon swung a hard right jab into Vic's face, catching him on the cheekbone. They two men were about evenly matched in size. The punch didn't knock Vic over, but it stopped his forward momentum and rocked him back on his heels. He countered with a body blow to the thug's ribs, fist meeting flesh with a meaty thud.

Erin saw that Vic had his hands full. She thought of going for her gun or her Taser, but there was too much chance of hitting her fellow detective. The guy Vic had thrown was climbing back over the bar with a beer bottle in his hand, looking to come in behind Vic, but he wasn't paying any attention to her. There were advantages to being small and female in a fight.

Erin came in low and fast. She knew she wasn't as big as most guys, so when she got in a fight she relied on her lower center of gravity and using her opponents' momentum against them. She looped an arm up under the thug's left arm and around his neck, used her hip as a pivot point, and flipped him. He went over backward with a startled squawk that turned into a groan as he hit the floor hard for the second time in less than ten seconds. He lay there, stunned, and she turned her attention to Vic's fight.

It lasted only a little longer. Vic was a classic boxer, a big guy who knew how to use his strength. He slammed a left-right-left combination into his opponent's stomach, doubling the man over. Then he brought down his right hand in a hammer-blow between the guy's shoulder blades, leaving him sprawled on the ground. Vic spun on his heel, fists cocked, ready to strike. He saw Erin and grinned.

"I'll get Frankie," she said.

"I've got these two," Vic agreed, pointing to the two prone men.

Erin didn't go straight after Frankie, however. She ran back the way she'd come. As she went, she keyed the remote control on Rolf's compartment, popping the door. The Shepherd was waiting. Trained and conditioned for moments like this, he hit the sidewalk ready for action.

"Rolf! *Komm hier!*" she ordered. The dog followed hard on her heels, back into Bernie's. Vic had already cuffed one of the goons and was on top of the other, a knee planted in the man's back, tightening a zip-tie as a temporary restraint. Erin and her K-9 raced past them and out the back.

They emerged into a back alley choked with trash and debris. Frankie Fingers had a good head start. Erin couldn't see him, had no idea which way he'd gone, and would've been lost on her own.

"Rolf! *Such!*" she said, giving the German command which meant "track."

Partnership with a K-9 relied foremost on training, on the endless hours human and dog spent working on commands and practice scenarios. But it also counted on something more intangible, the bond forged during that training. A K-9 couldn't just be passed off to another officer and function with anything like the same effectiveness. Rolf and Erin had worked together for three years, and she swore he could read her thoughts. If Rolf could talk, he might have explained the subtleties of her body language and tone of voice. But as it was, he caught the fresh smell of a frightened, agitated man and he was off on his appointed task.

Rolf went left, leapt a tipped-over trash can, slalomed around a couple of discarded packing crates, and came to a six-foot chain-link fence blocking the way. He tensed, jumped, and scrambled the rest of the way over the fence before Erin was halfway there. Erin lost sight of him as he hit the ground on the far side and went around a corner, but she knew he had the scent. He wouldn't stop until he ran down his quarry, or until he came to an obstacle he couldn't cross.

She ran after the dog. As she vaulted the fence and came down on the far side, she heard Rolf give a tremendous snarl, followed by a yell of fear and pain. She drew her gun as she rounded the corner, the snarls and cries continuing.

"Stop fighting my dog!" she shouted, then felt a little foolish when she saw what had happened. She was in a maintenance alley behind a row of seedy tenements. Thirty yards ahead was a fire escape. Frankie had tried to clamber up the rickety metal, but since the bottom of the escape was a drop-down ladder, he'd had to climb on top of a trash dumpster and jump for a handhold. He'd made the leap, but before he'd been able to pull himself the rest of the way up, Rolf had caught up with him. The K-9 had sprung to the top of the dumpster and launched himself at the tempting target of his target's dangling legs. Now Frankie hung from his fingertips with the strength of desperation as almost a hundred pounds of pissed-off police dog swung beneath him, teeth clamped firmly to the leg of his jeans. If the pants had been tight-fitting, they might have ripped and freed the escaping man, but they were loose, and so Rolf's weight was slowly pulling Frankie's pants off.

Erin was tempted to wait and see whether Frankie's grip or his trousers gave way first, but she didn't want to risk the man falling on top of her dog. She holstered her gun and pulled her Taser instead. "Frankie!" she shouted. "I'm going to call off my dog in a second. When I do, count to three and then let go. If you try anything else, I'm gonna zap your ass. Either way, you're hitting the ground."

"Sure! Whatever! Just get this crazy thing offa me!" was the agreeable reply.

"Rolf! *Pust! Hier!*" she called, ordering him to leave his target and return to her. Obedient to his training, he immediately released his hold on Frankie's leg, dropped to the pavement, and trotted back to Erin, tail wagging excitedly.

Frankie thought about making a run for it. Erin saw his arms tense. Her own finger went inside the trigger guard of her Taser and she sighted on his midsection. But he thought better of it and tumbled to the ground. He started to stand up, tripped over his tangled jeans, and went down again.

"Stay on the ground!" she snapped, though it was hard not to laugh at the man's predicament. "Get on your stomach! Spread your arms!"

All the fight had gone out of Frankie. He obeyed. She cuffed him, read him his rights, and searched him, looking for weapons and finding a knife with a four-inch folding blade. Then she got him back on his feet. They circled around the fence to come back into the bar from the front.

Vic looked up as she re-entered Bernie's, prisoner in tow, Rolf proudly pacing beside them. The two thugs were propped against the wall, seated on the floor, properly secured. The Russian detective saw Frankie struggling to pull up the seat of his pants and raised an eyebrow at Erin.

"I didn't think the two of you were out there that long," he said. "Couldn't it wait till you got off-duty?"

She rolled her eyes. "Rolf pulled his pants down with his teeth."

Vic's other eyebrow joined the first one. "Didn't know the dog was into that sort of thing."

Erin couldn't help smiling. "You've got no idea," she said.

"Let's get these three back to lockup."

"We'd better call a backup car," Vic said. "I don't think everyone's gonna fit." He had a point. Erin's Charger only had room for one prisoner in the back seat, the other half being taken up by Rolf's compartment.

"I'll call it in," she said.

"Hey, O'Reilly?"

"Yeah?"

"You're not half bad."

"Neither are you," Erin said. "I guess maybe you can tag along on my next collar."

"Oh, for Christ's sake," Frankie muttered. "Do you two have to make out while you're on the clock?"

"He resisting arrest?" Vic said, taking a step toward the man and curling one massive hand into a fist. "He looks like he's resisting arrest."

"Okay, okay! Jesus!" Frankie said, shutting up.

* * *

"I sent you out to talk to one guy," Webb said. "Catch-and-release. Now you've got him in my interrogation room, plus two more meatheads. Was there a bulk discount?"

"He ran," Vic said. "The other two got in the way, picked a fight."

The lieutenant glanced at Erin, who nodded. "He's right, sir. Fergus bolted the second Vic ID'd himself, and the others obstructed. Vic tossed one out of the way, and then the fight was on."

"Either of you get marked?"

"Nope," Vic said. "I took down one, Erin put the other on the floor. We didn't get hurt."

"You've got a bruise on your cheek," Webb observed. "You

want to press for felony assault?"

Vic shrugged and touched his swollen face, none too gently. "Forgot about that," he said. "We're running down Murder One. Maybe use the assault as leverage, get the mug to talk, but otherwise, I don't give a damn."

"Not a bad thought," Webb said. "You okay, O'Reilly?"

"Of course I am."

"That's a pretty big guy you were mixing it up with," he said. "You have to use the dog?"

She bristled at the implication. "Rolf was in the car," she said. "The guy rushed me and I gave him a hip-throw. He underestimated me, like a lot of guys do."

Webb let that one pass. "Okay, Fergus is definitely into something, or he wouldn't have run. O'Reilly, why don't you and I brace the goons and see what shakes loose? Then we'll lean on Frankie Fingers."

"Me, sir?" Erin said, startled.

Webb gave her a sour smile. "You're a detective, aren't you? This is what we do. You need to get a start sometime. I'll be running the interrogations. You can assist. Just follow my lead. Neshenko, Jones, you can watch."

Chapter 8

Thug Number One was named Damien Knox. He'd been in and out of the system ever since being placed in a foster home at age eleven, moving through Juvie into half a dozen arrests and three short sentences for assault and disorderly conduct. Webb handed Erin a bulging police file with the particulars on the way down to the interrogation room. She tried to scan the relevant information, feeling rushed. Her body was still hopping with adrenaline and she had trouble concentrating on written words. It struck her that Webb probably knew this and that the whole thing was some sort of test.

When they got to the interrogation room, Webb didn't go straight in. He went into the observation room with the other detectives. There was a one-way mirror taking up a whole wall. On the other side, Erin saw the guy she'd thrown in the fight. He sat slouched in a plain metal chair, a chain linking his cuffed wrists to the table. His expression was somewhere between boredom and exasperation.

"You always want to take a minute to look over your man before bracing him," Webb said. "See if he's nervous or calm, angry or sad. You can use all that in your approach. How's he look to you?"

"Seems pretty cool," Erin said.

"And what's that tell you?"

"He's been in these rooms before."

"You already knew that from his file," Webb said. "What else?"

She thought about the guys she'd brought in over her years on patrol. "I kicked his ass a little while ago. He's feeling silly for getting slapped around by a girl, so he's making up for it by acting tough."

"We can use that," Webb said. "Now, remember, we don't really want Knox. We want Frankie."

"Got it."

"Okay, Detective," he said. "Put on your game face."

Knox looked up as they entered, trying to hold his look of bored annoyance, but Erin didn't miss the way his eyes flicked nervously at her. He stayed slumped down in his chair, but his shoulders and neck were tense.

"Damien Knox," Webb said conversationally. "I'm Lieutenant Webb. You've met Detective O'Reilly already." He pulled out a chair on the other side of the table from the man and sat down. Erin remained standing against the wall beside the door, arms crossed. Webb's whole manner was nonchalant, managing to convey a sense of casual disregard. It was calculated to poke at Knox's pride. In Knox's world, Erin knew, respect was the most valuable coin.

"It's been a while since we've had you in here," Webb continued, not even bothering to look directly at him. "I guess you just haven't been important enough to waste our time."

Knox glared at him. "Screw you, man. Do I get a lawyer?"

"You asking for one?" Webb asked. "I don't think you need legal counsel. You're not worth it."

Knox shot a look Erin's way, and even before he opened his

mouth, she realized why Webb had brought her into the room. It wasn't just as a learning experience. She could've learned as much from the observation room next door. The Lieutenant was deliberately provoking Knox, knowing a violent, arrogant young man was more likely to slip up in the presence of a woman who'd smacked him down. Knox would want to impress her, display his plumage like an underworld peacock.

"Then what the hell am I doing here?" Knox snapped.

"You assaulted a police officer... at least, you tried to," Webb said.

"Hey, I never did nothing to her," Knox retorted.

"You don't have to be competent," Webb said. "Taking the swing was enough to place you in violation of New York's Penal Code, Section 120.08. O'Reilly, would you enlighten our guest as to this section of the code?"

Like any patrol officer, Erin knew that part of the state's code by heart. "Assault on a peace officer, police officer, fireman, or emergency services personnel," she recited.

"I never touched you!" he protested.

"That's because I tossed you on your ass," she said, smiling with artificial sweetness.

"You did some kind of sneaky judo move when I came at you!" he said. "In a fair fight I'd knock your teeth out!"

"Okay," Webb said. "You've just confessed to a Class C violent felony. That's worth a maximum of... what, O'Reilly?"

"Up to fifteen years."

"Right. Fifteen years," Webb said. He made direct eye contact with Knox for the first time in the conversation. "So maybe I was wrong, Mr. Knox. Maybe you're worth our time after all."

Knox was sitting up straight now, and Erin saw sweat beading on his forehead. "Hey now," he said. "I didn't hurt her."

"That's good," Webb said, his voice becoming soothing, the

voice of a concerned man with nothing but the best intentions. "And I may be able to help you dig yourself out of the hole you're in. But for me to help you, you have to help me."

"What do you want, asshole?" Knox demanded, trying to cover his fear with defiance. It didn't work. Erin didn't need a nose like Rolf's to sense the fear radiating out of this guy. He was all bluff and brag, no real courage.

Webb ignored the insult. "I want to know about William O'Connell."

"Fourth-Place Billy?" Knox blinked. "What for?"

"Why do you call him that?" Webb asked.

Knox laughed nervously. "He likes horse-racing," he explained. "But he's no good at picking winners."

"Of course," Webb said. "Do you play the ponies, Damien?"

"No way, man. Good way to lose all your money."

Webb nodded understandingly. "Poor Billy lost a lot, didn't he?"

Knox nodded along with the detective, relieved at the innocuous turn to the conversation.

"He owed money to a bunch of guys," Webb went on. "One of them was Frankie Fingers."

"So? Lotsa guys owe Frankie."

"Yeah, Frankie's in on a lot of action," Webb said.

"What about it?" Knox challenged. "Yeah, guys get in to Frankie for a few large. He lets 'em run up a little credit line."

"How's he do his collections?" Webb said. "When that credit line runs out?"

"Gary and me help him out sometimes," Knox said, referring to Thug Number Two, Gary Morgan. "So does Billy."

Erin was having trouble following the thread of Webb's thinking, but this revelation caught her attention. William O'Connell hadn't just owed money to Fergus, he'd been working for him.

Webb must have been as surprised as she was, but he didn't show it. "Yeah," the lieutenant said. "He'd go around to talk to them when they got too far behind, flash his piece, make sure they got the message?"

"Yeah," Knox agreed.

"Slap them around a little to put some sense into them?" Webb suggested.

"Nah, Billy was no good for that," Knox said. "You ever see the guy? Any muscle work, you'd want Gary or me."

Erin couldn't believe what she was hearing. There was a hardened criminal in front of her, confessing to more and more crimes, all for what? To recover his image after being beaten up by a woman half his size. She'd always considered her small stature and gender as disadvantages in her profession, but she was re-evaluating that conclusion.

"So if the debtor won't pay up when Billy comes calling, Frankie sends you in to take care of business," Webb said, taking care not to mention that O'Connell was in no condition to make further collection calls. "Good idea. You look like a guy who knows how to convince people."

Absurdly pleased, Knox preened a little in his seat. "Nobody wants to mess with me," he said.

"I expect you get paid pretty well for that work," Webb said.

"We get a percentage," Knox said. "It's a commission, like."

"Does Billy make the same percentage?"

"Nah," Knox said. "He's working off debt."

Webb nodded. "How much does he owe Frankie?"

Knox shrugged. "Dunno. I don't keep track of that shit."

Webb stood up. "Thanks, Damien. I appreciate the help. If you can keep this good attitude, I think we can work something out with the D.A. I've got some other things to take care of, so why don't you just relax a little. You a coffee drinker?"

"It any good?" Knox asked.

"It's police coffee, so it tastes like shit, but it's strong," Webb said with a friendly smile.

"Sure, why not?"

"I'll have a cup brought in," Webb said.

Damien sat back in his chair as the lieutenant motioned Erin to the door with a sideways tilt of his head.

*   *   *

"Morgan next?" Erin asked, once they were in the hallway.

Webb nodded. "Let's do this. You and me, just like before. Jones, Neshenko, you can observe again. Anyone have any questions? You clear on what we're doing?"

"We're looking for corroboration," Jones said.

"Exactly," Webb said. "We get him to support what Knox just said, we see if anything else pops, then we see what we can squeeze out of Fergus. But we need to be flexible. If another avenue opens up, we'll take that and see where it leads."

When they looked through the one-way glass at Gary Morgan, Erin saw the differences between him and Knox right away. Knox had tried to be cool, pretending that getting beaten up and arrested was something that happened to him all the time. Morgan looked terrible. His face was pale, his eyes hollow. He hunched over the table in the interrogation room, holding his stomach. Erin wondered just how hard Vic had hit him, and hoped the guy wasn't seriously injured. He'd seemed fine earlier, when they'd brought him in. Now she could see sweat running down his face.

"We need a different approach here," Webb said. "How's he look to you?"

"Like hell," she said.

"Yeah," Webb said. "Neshenko, what'd you do to him?"

"A couple to the gut, one on the back when he folded over," Vic said with a shrug. "He's fine."

"Remind me never to get in a fistfight with you," Jones said.

"Okay," Webb said. "Here we go." He opened the door and went in, Erin on his heels.

"Gary Morgan, I'm Lieutenant Webb, NYPD," the lieutenant said. "This is Detective O'Reilly. We need to talk to you. We'd like to help you, and we hope you can help us."

The prisoner's eyes darted back and forth between the two of them. "I need protection, man," he said.

It wasn't what either of them was expecting. Erin felt her mouth open, with no idea what was going to come out. Webb, more used to interrogations, just raised an eyebrow. "From what?" he asked, his voice giving nothing away.

"They're gonna kill us," Morgan said.

Erin realized that the man wasn't in pain, at least nothing serious. He was scared.

Webb leaned forward, his face earnest. "We can protect you," he said. "But to do that, I need you to tell me who's coming after you."

"The same guys who got Billy," Morgan said.

"You heard what happened to Billy?" Webb asked.

"Yeah," Morgan nodded emphatically. "I got a call from a guy, he told me Billy got whacked this morning."

"You discuss this with Frankie and Damien?" Webb asked.

"Nah, man, I was about to when that bitch and her partner busted in."

"So you and Billy were in it together," Webb said, giving no indication of what "it" was, letting Morgan fill in the blanks himself.

"It's crazy, man," Morgan said. "We weren't into anything heavy. Nothing you'd think a guy would get killed for. Crazy, like, out of their minds."

Webb leaned even further forward. "Who's crazy enough to blow up Billy?" he pressed.

"Cars, man," Morgan whispered, and for a second Erin had no idea what he was talking about. Then she remembered the nickname.

"Cars Carlyle," she said aloud.

Morgan nodded again. "Yeah, him! Dude's quiet and calm, like, but he's nuts. I heard he killed a guy in a barfight once, just beat his head in with a chair leg, for nothing! And he blows shit up, too, with this homemade shit he makes, like, in his basement!"

"He's got a bomb lab in his basement?" Webb asked, his expression polite skepticism.

"Well, maybe not the basement," Morgan said. "But he makes bombs! And he's out to get everybody on Frankie's crew!"

"What for?" Webb asked.

"I don't know!" Morgan almost screamed it out. "Maybe he wants Frankie's book. Maybe Frankie just pissed him off. Ask Frankie. You gotta help me, man!"

To the surprise and embarrassment of both detectives, Morgan began to cry, snuffling and dribbling snot. Webb glanced at Erin. She shrugged. Webb stood up.

"Thanks for the information, Gary," he said, his tone compassionate. "We'll look into Carlyle. And don't worry. Nobody's going to blow you up, as long as you're here with us. I'll have them bring in some coffee. Just sit tight for a bit. I'll be back."

*   *   *

In the hallway again, the detectives congregated. Webb leaned back against the wall and rubbed the bridge of his nose. "What the hell is going on?" he muttered.

"Turf war?" Vic guessed.

"Civil war in the O'Malleys," Erin suggested. "Carlyle and Fergus both run sports books. Maybe Frankie was crowding Carlyle's territory, like Vic's thinking, and Carlyle hit one of his collection guys."

"You think that means he's planning to take out the others, too?" Webb asked.

She thought it over. "No, I don't," she said. "It wouldn't make sense. O'Connell doesn't exactly seem like the toughest guy in the Irish mob. If you were going to take down this crew, why start with him and put the others on guard?"

Jones nodded. "Especially if you're using bombs," she said. "Why not bomb the bar where these guys hang out instead? Take them all out at once."

"Is it enough for a warrant on Carlyle?" Vic asked, cocking his head at the interrogation room's door. "What he said?"

Webb shook his head. "No, way too thin. He doesn't even have a good reason why Carlyle would try a hit. He's heard Carlyle's a scary S.O.B., but it all sounds like street gossip and trash talk. He's never seen Carlyle's bomb shop, if it even exists."

"What if we lean on Fergus? He might have something," Jones said.

"Yeah, we'll try," Webb said. "Jones, you're with me on this one. O'Reilly, you and Neshenko watch."

"Sir…" Erin began, then stopped.

"Something wrong, Detective?" Webb asked with a raised eyebrow and an expression of mild interest.

"No, sir," she said, bottling up her irritation. She'd wanted to protest being sidelined for this interrogation, the most important one of the three, but she'd remembered she was the least experienced detective on the squad. You didn't pinch-hit with a rookie when the game was on the line; you went with your proven sluggers.

*　*　*

"Does it bother you?" Erin asked Vic. She stood beside him in the observation room, staring through the glass at Franklin Fergus. Webb and Jones were conferring outside, getting ready to get the ball rolling.

"What?" Vic asked.

"Getting benched."

Vic shrugged. "We can't all go in there. I'll get my turn. Hey, I got to beat down a scumbag, so it's not a bad day for me."

"You," she said, "are a brutality lawsuit waiting to happen."

He shrugged again. "I followed the rules. Morgan hit me before I put him on the floor. Anyway, these guys are assholes. You think *they're* going to sue the department? For what? They didn't even break anything."

Erin shook her head. "Vic, you've got to watch yourself. You can't go beating up all the thugs you meet."

"Hey, if I see Rodney King, I'll cut him some slack," Vic said. Then, seeing that she didn't smile, he spread his hands. "Come on, Erin. You were there. Frankie ran for it, these two jailbirds jumped in front of us. I might've chucked the one guy a little hard, but he'll be fine. He got up fast enough, till you dropped him again. We didn't start this."

She sighed. "Yeah, you're right this time, and I admit it, that was pretty satisfying."

"Quiet," Vic said. "The show's starting."

Webb and Jones had entered. Frankie Fergus sat in his chair, looking as comfortable as a guy could who'd been dragged off a fire escape by a German Shepherd.

Webb didn't waste any time. He waded in right away. "Listen up, Frankie," he snapped. He walked up to the table, planted his hands on the tabletop, and put his face as close to

Fergus as possible. "Your guys are getting whacked out there. Fourth-Place Billy was the first to go, and Morgan thinks he's next. What do you think?"

Erin was watching her commanding officer, trying to pick up whatever she could from his body language for future usage, so she almost missed Frankie's reaction. The thug had pretty good self-control compared with his underlings, but his eyes went wide, his jaw tightened, and every muscle in his arms and shoulders tensed. He didn't say anything, but Webb had his full attention.

"Oh, you didn't know about Billy?" Webb asked. He hadn't missed the signs of surprise, either. "Look, Frankie, I know you're making gambling book. But I'm with Major Crimes, not Vice. I don't give a damn if you're running numbers. But when someone's blowing your people up, that's my business. So if you want to sit there and do that whole silent interrogation bit, fine by me, but I'll be standing over here sizing up your ass for my size twelve boot."

Erin saw something strange. As Webb was talking, Fergus relaxed. He'd regained his equilibrium, or else something the Lieutenant had said had calmed him down. The momentum in the room shifted toward the guy in the chair.

"Who's Fourth-Place Billy?" Fergus asked, his face showing childish innocence.

"You know damn well who he is," Webb said. "And I've got two guys who've already told me he works for you. So cut the crap."

"Oh, right, *that* Billy," Fergus said. "Geez, somebody killed him? That's terrible!"

Webb hit the table with his fist and glared at the other man. "That's right, keep jerking me around," he growled. "See what happens."

Jones stepped forward. She'd been standing by the door,

watching the confrontation. Now she laid a hand on Webb's elbow. "Sir, please," she said.

Webb stood back, breathing heavily, scowling at Fergus. Jones sat down opposite the prisoner and began talking in a quiet, reasonable tone.

"Mr. Fergus, I'm sorry about this," she said. "Lieutenant Webb is upset because he's worried more people are going to get hurt. The bomb that killed Billy could easily have done a lot more damage. His wife could have been in the car, too. Or the bomb could have malfunctioned and gone off late, on a crowded street. I need your help, Mr. Fergus."

"I don't help cops," he said, folding his arms.

"I need you to help yourself," Jones said. "Billy was your guy. Anyone who went after him is going to be looking at you as the next good target. You're a big guy with the Irish. You know all the major players. You must have some idea who's moving in on you. Solve your problem, and let's get this guy taken care of before he puts another bomb somewhere... like under your bar."

Fergus stared at her for a long moment. "I've never seen a cop with blue hair before," he finally said. "They let you wear it like that?"

She smiled. "I used to work the gang unit," she said. "It helped me blend in."

"Really?" he said, giving her a once-over. "Aren't you a little small for that kind of work?"

"The last guy I busted said the same thing, right before I slapped the cuffs on him."

Fergus grinned. "That so? Damn, girl."

"I know how the game works," she said. "So what do you say?"

"Okay, listen, you didn't hear this from me," he said. "But you want to look close at Cars Carlyle. And that's all I've got to say."

*   *   *

"Well, that was interesting," Webb said. The detectives had gone back upstairs to Major Crimes. Rolf welcomed Erin with a businesslike sniff and wag of his tail, then settled back down beside her desk.

"So where are we, sir?" Vic asked.

The lieutenant shrugged. He went to the whiteboard against the wall and wrote MORTON CARLYLE under the heading SUSPECTS.

"I don't know, sir," Erin said.

"What don't you know, O'Reilly?" Webb demanded. "His name is all over this thing. O'Connell owed him money. O'Connell worked for a competitor of his in the Irish Mob. He's a bomb-maker, for God's sake."

"Yeah, but Skip Taylor said the bomb wasn't placed by a pro," she said. "There's something we're missing here."

"You think we shouldn't be looking at Carlyle?"

"I like Carlyle for this," Vic said.

"Me, too," Jones said, but she sounded less certain.

"We absolutely need to look at him," Erin said. "That wasn't what I meant. I just think there's more to the case. What about Frankie?"

"What about him?" Vic asked.

"Can we hold him?"

"For resisting arrest," Webb said. "But that's all we've got on him for now. No, I think he walks, unless we find anything else to pin on him."

"Why'd he run?" Erin demanded.

"Guys like that run from cops," Jones said. "It's a habit, practically a reflex."

"Were you really on the gang squad?" Vic asked her.

"Yeah, before I went to IA," she said. "I used to dress up like a ganger girl, go to all the cool parties, try to steer young bangers away from the life."

"Wish I could've seen that," Vic said. "You wanna show me your tats sometime?"

"In your lonely dreams, big boy."

"Sir?" Erin said to Webb. "Everything okay?"

Webb looked blank. "What do you mean?"

"I thought he was getting to you."

He laughed. "Good cop, bad cop," he said. "Jones and I worked it out ahead of time."

"It worked, I guess," Erin said. "You got the name. But we don't really have anything more on Carlyle."

"It's still not enough for a warrant," Webb agreed. "But it's enough to go talk to him again."

"I'll do it," Erin said quickly.

Webb looked at her curiously. "Okay, if you want it. Neshenko, you want to go with her?"

"I'd rather go alone," she said.

"Why?" Vic challenged.

"Something he said," Erin explained. "He... he knew my dad. I think maybe he'll talk to me, maybe say a little more if it's just me."

Webb considered it. "Okay," he said again. "But be careful. These are dangerous guys we're dealing with here. I want Neshenko close by. Anything smells hinky, you get him in there."

"It's a bar in downtown Manhattan," Erin said. "It's not like I'm following the guy down a dark alley."

"Yeah," Vic said. "And no Irish cop ever got in trouble walking into a bar."

Chapter 9

Dealing with Fergus and his goons had eaten up most of the day. It was late afternoon by the time Erin got to the Barley Corner. Vic stayed outside, lounging in the car. She debated the wisdom of bringing Rolf into the pub. He helped her confidence with his presence, and he'd be essential if there was trouble, but he also might make Carlyle nervous. She decided to leave the dog with Vic. "Don't eat him, boy," she told Rolf, rubbing his ears. The Shepherd gave her a long, doubtful stare as she closed the car door.

The smell of roast beef and potatoes inside the Corner made her mouth water. Her stomach growled, and she suddenly remembered she'd skipped lunch. With all the excitement of chasing down Fergus, she'd clean forgotten to eat. But that would have to wait.

The Corner was starting to fill up with the first wave of drinkers, the guys who'd gotten off work early. The ratio of men to women was about eight to one, even more lopsided if she didn't count the waitresses. Most of the guys were big, blue-collar types. It was a lot like the bars she was used to in Queens.

Erin looked around, but didn't see Carlyle. His silver hair

and neat attire should have made him stand out. Momentarily stymied, she eased her way up to the bar. With that magic every good bartender knows, Danny materialized in front of her.

"Afternoon, ma'am," he said. "What'll it be?"

Erin wanted a drink. Maybe it was the atmosphere of the place, maybe it was nerves, maybe it was just her Irish heritage coming out at an inconvenient moment, but she very nearly asked for a shot of whiskey. Then she reminded herself she was on duty. "Coke," she said.

"Anything to stiffen it?"

"No, thanks. Just Coke."

He filled a glass and set it down on the bar. "Cash or tab?"

"Cash," she said, reaching for her wallet.

"Please, love, allow me," a voice at her elbow said in a rich Irish brogue. "Just put it on my tab, Danny."

Erin thought for an instant it was Carlyle. The accent was nearly identical, that of a man born in Northern Ireland. But even before she turned to face him, she knew it came from a different man. There was a kind of reckless amusement in the voice. It was made for laughing and singing. The face of the man beside her was a perfect match for his tone. He was just an inch or so taller than Erin, so she was looking right into his eyes. They were a bright, brilliant green, laugh lines crinkling their corners. He had a slender face dotted with a few freckles, framed by thick, wavy hair of such a fiery red that she suspected a dye job. He had a warm, conspiratorial smile that made her think of shared secrets.

"Sure thing, Corky," Danny said.

"Thanks," Erin said. "But I don't accept drinks from strangers."

The newcomer grinned. "Of course you don't, love, which is why I appreciate your making an exception in my case. You're far too fair a lass to be drinking alone. Danny, if you wouldn't mind another Glen D for me, while I keep the lady company?"

A glass of whiskey appeared in front of Erin's new drinking companion. He held it up and cocked it toward her. "Amber poison, love," he said. "You know why the good Lord invented whiskey and hangovers, don't you? Without them, the Irish would long ago have conquered the world." He sipped the drink and sighed appreciatively. "Ah, that's fine. You surprise me, though. I'd pegged you for a whiskey lass yourself. Or haven't you any Irish in you?"

"On both sides," she admitted. "But I can't drink right now."

He raised an eyebrow. "I find it hard to believe an Irish lass would come into a public house solely for the purpose of *not* taking a drink."

"I'm here on business, Mr...?"

He shook his head. "Not Mister anything, love. James Corcoran, Corky to my friends, of which I hope you will be a dear one. Will you favor me with your name?"

"*Detective* Erin O'Reilly," she said, emphasizing her title.

"Oh, grand!" he exclaimed, more amused and impressed than intimidated. "You'd not be the first copper to wet your whistle on the clock, and I'd not tell a soul, but I understand. So what brings you here, Erin?"

Corcoran was standing just a bit too close, giving off all the signs of a man looking for a date, but that didn't bother Erin by itself. She dealt with that sort of thing all the time. What made it awkward was that she liked the look of him. He practically dripped with charisma. She was sure he'd be a fun guy to hang out with, the life of every party. And she was unattached at the moment. But she was on a murder investigation, not enjoying an evening off, and she needed to keep her mind on her job. She'd been a detective less than forty-eight hours, and she wasn't going to start flirting with some random guy when she was supposed to be interviewing a potential suspect. Especially a random guy who was hanging out in a mob bar.

"I need to talk to Mr. Carlyle," she said.

"And why would a copper need to be talking to him?"

"Police business," she said. She glanced around again and still didn't see Carlyle.

"Ah, to be sure," he said. "And after you've concluded your business, would you be letting a lad buy you a more interesting drink?"

She had to smile at his persistence. "Not tonight, Mr. Corcoran."

"I suppose I'll have to live in hope, Erin," he said. "But so that we're clear, I'm quite certain you'd take me up on my offer in other circumstances."

Erin gave him a level, hard stare, the one she reserved for juvenile delinquents. "How sure are you?"

The glare bounced off with no apparent effect. "Sure enough that I'll be certain to have our next encounter under more relaxed conditions. I think you're worth pursuing, Erin, and I think a copper might like being the one pursued for a change." He looked into her eyes with a frank warmth, then flicked his gaze past her. "Ah, and we were getting on so well. There's the lad you came to speak with."

Erin turned to see Carlyle, who'd just emerged from the back of the pub. She glanced at her companion, but James Corcoran had slipped into the crowd and vanished. It was an impressively quick fade. She put Corcoran out of her mind. Carlyle was the whole reason she was here. She gulped down the last half of her Coke, a poor substitute for liquid courage, and stood up.

Carlyle made eye contact when they were about ten feet apart. He smiled with surprising warmth. Erin didn't return it. Now that she was face-to-face with him again, she wondered why she'd volunteered for this, and why she'd come alone. Up close, she remembered how she'd felt at their last meeting. She thought of her conversation with her father, of the way Carlyle had played him. Her hands clenched into fists at her sides.

"A good evening to you, Miss O'Reilly," he said, offering his hand.

She stared at it for a moment, making up her mind, then gave him a quick, abrupt handshake.

"I confess," he continued, "I wasn't expecting to see you again so soon. I'm pleased my establishment made such a fine impression on you."

"Mr. Carlyle, this isn't a social call."

"I never thought for a moment that it was."

Erin buried a flash of irritation. The guy was so *smooth*. Everything bounced off him. She decided to play it cool, just like he was doing. "But it's a fine bar," she said. "If I wasn't on duty, I might still drop by."

"Ah, grand!" he exclaimed, sounding just like Corcoran. "You'll be welcome at any time. I'm always proud to cater to New York's finest."

"And here I was thinking this was a mob bar," she said, just to see how he'd react.

Carlyle spread his hands in a gesture of innocence. "You wound me, Miss O'Reilly. My public house is open and welcome to anyone who cares to come through the doors. You'll see no secret business conducted here. Why would I have anything to hide from you or your colleagues?"

Bullshit, Erin thought. "I'm glad to hear it," was what she said. "I'm hoping there's something you can help me with."

"Any favor I can do for you will be my pleasure."

A shiver ran down Erin's spine at that, remembering her father's last words to her. "It's not a personal favor," she said. "It's for the city of New York."

Carlyle sat down beside her on a bar stool that hadn't been

empty until a moment ago. The big, beefy guy who'd been sitting there had quietly moved off the instant Carlyle had looked his way. "Miss O'Reilly, I do no business with cities," he said. "I'm a publican. My business is retail, man-to-man, man-to-woman. I'm not talking to New York City, I'm talking to you."

"Okay, Mr. Carlyle," she said, meeting his stare. "Let's talk. First off, William O'Connell owed you money. That's not speculation, that's a fact."

"Let's suppose for the sake of argument you're speaking truth," he said.

"How were you planning on getting repaid?"

Carlyle drummed his fingers on the bar's dark, worn wood. "In full, and with interest."

"Could you elaborate?"

"Were a lad to owe me, say, sixty thousand dollars, he would make payments in monthly installments, at fifteen percent," Carlyle said. "Still speaking hypothetically, of course. It'd not be in my best interests to blast him to bits. Why kill a man making good on his debts? That would be killing the goose that laid the proverbial golden eggs. Then, I'd also have to consider the example it might set for others who might owe money."

"That's true enough," Erin admitted. "But there's also the little fact of Billy working for your competitor."

Carlyle didn't react, except to raise a finger to signal the bartender. "Pour me a house special, Danny," he said. "It's appropriate to the conversation. And what can I get for you, Miss O'Reilly? You needn't worry about cost, it's on the house."

"Nothing, thanks."

Danny brought Carlyle a glass of Guinness, then dropped the bomb shot of Irish cream and whiskey into it. Carlyle knocked back the drink in a matter of seconds, bringing the empty glass down on the bar with a thud. The shot glass bounced against the inside of the beer glass with a follow-up clink.

The Irishman turned back to Erin. "I'm well aware O'Connell was working for Mr. Fergus," he said. "Apparently, he owed dear Franklin even more than whatever he may have owed to me. What of it?"

"Look, Mr. Carlyle," she said. "You've got a history here. You worked for the O'Malley gang down in Queens back in the '90s, blowing up garbage trucks. Now you've got a rival who's had one of his enforcers blown up in a car bomb. Maybe he was paying you, maybe he wasn't. Maybe you were just pissed at him. All I know is, right now I've got a list of suspects exactly one name long." She thought of Webb in the interrogation room. "I'm not asking you to help me. I'm asking you to help yourself. Because the way the wind is blowing right now, this thing's going to get hung on you."

Carlyle smiled. "So you're saying it's in my best interests to help you... unless I blew poor William to atoms, of course, in which case I've honestly no idea what you want me to say. Would you be wanting a written confession, should I prove to be the perpetrator?"

"What do *you* want, Mr. Carlyle?" she shot back.

"At the moment? To share a drink with a charming lass while engaged in pleasant conversation. What more could a lad ask?"

"Don't you want to clear your name?"

"Miss O'Reilly, if my name was clear before this business crossed your path, I very much doubt you'd be consulting me on the matter," he said. "What's my occupation?"

"You're a gangster, *Cars*," she said, emphasizing his nickname.

"You're a copper. We're all playing our parts in this game. You're seeking information. It would be a sight easier, I'll admit, if you could simply drag me to the local jail in irons. But you'd prefer to collar the true guilty party, wouldn't you? Now, I'm not saying I'd anything to do with those trucks that exploded in Queens all those years ago..."

"Of course not," she said dryly.

"...but I do know a thing or two about explosive devices. This information may be helpful to you. Perhaps we're in a position to assist one another."

"Maybe. But you still haven't told me what you want from the NYPD," she said.

Carlyle shook his head. "As I've said, I do business with people."

"Okay, then. What do you want from me?"

He was still smiling. "A free exchange of thoughts. Not a string attached. Here and now, I'd like to talk about bombs, and I imagine you do as well. So can we lay aside whatever you think you know about me, and get on with solving your little explosive problem?"

"Okay, start talking," she said. At least it would get him talking about the case.

"Do you know how the device was detonated?"

"It was hooked up to the ignition."

"So the lad was blasted when he started the engine?"

Erin wondered how much she should be sharing with this guy. "I didn't say that."

"Was there a cellular telephone?"

"Yeah, he had a phone."

"Not on the victim," he said. "Attached to the bomb."

"No."

"No remote detonator at all?"

She shook her head.

"A direct device," Carlyle said. "If you're wanting to kill a lad with a bomb, there's good and bad sides to such a thing. The benefit of it is, you needn't be present to do away with him. You can be halfway across town, enjoying a right lovely alibi. But like poison, such a bomb doesn't care who it kills."

"What's your point?" Erin asked.

"My point is, you're making some assumptions."

"Such as?"

"How do you know dear William was the intended target?"

Erin blinked. "Well, it was his car..."

"I suppose that proves him the target," Carlyle said quietly. "Unless, of course, someone else also had use of the automobile."

Her mind raced. She'd just made a connection. "The wife," she said quietly.

"Beg pardon?"

"She had a garden club meeting yesterday morning," Erin said. "She said she'd have to call for a cab. Which meant she'd been intending to drive..."

She stood up without finishing her thought. "Thanks," she said. "I have to go."

"Of course you do," he said, smiling. "I'm glad to be of service. Please do come back soon. I shall look forward to it." He stood in a gesture of old-world chivalry. "Good evening."

She was already heading out the door, pulling her phone and dialing Webb.

*   *   *

"Well?" Webb asked as soon as she identified herself. "What did the Irish bomb-maker have to say for himself?"

"It wasn't him. O'Connell, I mean," Erin said.

"You mean Carlyle didn't kill O'Connell?"

"No. Yes. I mean... I'm pretty sure Carlyle's not our guy. But O'Connell may not be our victim, either."

"O'Reilly? You're not making sense. Of course O'Connell's

the victim. He's dead, isn't he?"

She took a deep breath and started over. "Yeah, O'Connell got blown up. But the bomb might've been meant for someone else. The wife."

"The garden club meeting." Webb caught up fast.

"Yeah, she was going to drive that morning. Either the killer screwed up the schedule, or he meant to take out Cynthia."

"Yeah," Webb said. Then, gaining conviction, "Yeah. It fits. But the Irish Mob angle has to be there. Listen, O'Reilly. Are you absolutely certain Carlyle didn't plant the bomb?"

"No," she admitted. "But my gut says he didn't do it. Skip said it was an amateur device, and Carlyle's a pro. And then there was the way he was talking about it. He was cagey, but he seemed to be trying to help. I can't get a clear read on him. I think he's jerking me around a little, just for fun. I think…"

"What?"

"I think he likes me."

"A good cop can't get in bed with the Mob," Webb said dryly.

Erin bristled. "That wasn't what I meant, and you damn well know it. Sir."

"If he likes the way you look, you can use that to your advantage," he said. "But keep your head in the game."

"I never said he liked how I looked," she said in a low, tight voice. "I said he liked *me*."

"Whatever," Webb said. "Look, it's getting late. Touch base with Neshenko, then head home. This should keep overnight."

Erin wanted to be off the phone. She didn't like the implication that she might be open to Carlyle's manipulation. But a thought suddenly hit her. "Unless whoever was trying to kill Mrs. O'Connell makes another try."

"Damn," Webb said. "If she was targeted in order to threaten her husband, that's off the table." He sighed. "But I suppose we can't take the chance. I'll have Patrol send a car to babysit her. That should keep a lid on things till morning."

"If you say so, sir. We'll pick this up tomorrow, I guess."

"Good work, O'Reilly," Webb said. "You're shaping up into a decent detective."

She bit back a sarcastic retort and signed off. Then she walked to the car, where her two partners, old and new, were waiting for her. Rolf was excited to see her. Vic just looked bored.

"He our guy?" Vic asked as she got in.

"Nope," Erin said.

"Damn." Vic shrugged and eased his seat back. He didn't ask anything else and Erin, her thoughts busy replaying the conversation with Carlyle, didn't offer.

Chapter 10

Erin expected to have trouble sleeping. She hardly tasted her dinner, and almost completely zoned out her TV while thinking about the case, but she was more tired than she realized. The next thing she knew after climbing into bed, her alarm was buzzing. Rolf knew the sound well. By the time she sat up he was already on his feet, tongue hanging out, tail wagging.

She felt refreshed and ready to take on the case. Things were starting to shake loose, she could feel it. She hurried through her morning routine, still feeling strange to be working the daytime shift, and headed for the subway. She didn't have permission yet to take the Charger home with her; some bullshit paperwork needed to be filled out, and she hadn't had time to work through it.

Jones was already in the office, tapping away at her computer. "Morning," she said, pointing to the coffee machine.

Erin shook her head. "I had a cup at home."

"Probably better that way," Jones said, taking a sip from her own cup and grimacing. "You know, we keep giving this to the scumbags we interrogate, we're gonna get sued by the ACLU."

"Any of the others here yet?" Erin asked, sliding into her chair. Rolf flopped down beside her desk and planted his face between his paws.

"Nah," Jones said. "Vic usually turns up a couple minutes late, and the Lieutenant's a little sluggish before he gets his coffee in him."

"What about the Captain?"

"He's meeting with the Chief uptown," Jones said. "Progress report on the bombing."

"Really?" Erin wasn't happy to hear that. "Is there a lot of pressure coming down the line?"

Jones shrugged. "Always. But that's what the Captain's there for. He's a firewall to protect us from the political guys."

"I'd rather be working cases," Erin said.

"So would he," Jones laughed. "Anyway, what've you got? You and Vic get anything on Carlyle?"

"Not exactly," Erin said. She explained her conversation with the Irishman. Jones listened carefully, jotting down notes.

"Y'know, gang cases are a lot like working Internal Affairs," Jones said.

"How's that?"

"You can't break them just on the physical evidence," Jones explained. "There's two things that bring down mob operations. There's the money trail, and there's the human factor. You want to find someone who's weak and then flip him."

"Okay," Erin said. "But I get the feeling O'Connell was the weakest link in the O'Malleys, and he's our victim. Webb cracked open Fergus's two goons yesterday, but it didn't do us much good. I don't think they really know anything."

"So we follow the money," Jones said.

"What money?"

"Exactly." Jones went to the whiteboard and circled Cynthia O'Connell's name. "Let's suppose your informant is right." She wrote a question mark next to Cynthia and the word "victim" in front of it.

"Who wants her dead?" Erin wondered.

"Wrong question," Jones said. "If mob guys killed everyone they wanted dead, we'd be scooping up bodies by the truckload every Monday morning. It's not a matter of wanting. The question is, what's the payoff?"

"She didn't have money," Erin said. "Remember the apartment? They'd had to move out of their bigger place. It was packed with all sorts of random crap."

"Insurance," Jones said.

Erin nodded. "But didn't you look at insurance already?"

Jones scoffed. "I looked at William, since he was the one who'd gotten blown up. He had a little policy, twenty grand. Pocket change. It'd cover the funeral if the wife did it on the cheap."

"You think she took him out anyway?" Erin said. "It was pretty obvious she hated him."

"Maybe," Jones said. "But maybe..." She trailed off.

They looked at each other. The same thought hit both of them at once.

"Holy shit," Erin said.

Jones nodded. "I'm not sure this is a murder investigation anymore," she said.

"Nope," Erin said. "I think maybe we've got a really clumsy accidental suicide."

They couldn't help smiling at the dark humor of it. When Webb came up the stairs, looking bleary, they were still smiling. "What'd I miss?" he asked, taking in their amusement.

"I think we've got our bomber," Erin said.

"And there's even better news," Jones snickered. "It was a one-time thing. He's definitely not going to set off any more bombs."

Webb looked back and forth between them. "You solved the case in the first..." he glanced at the clock, "...ten minutes of the shift?"

"Not completely," Erin said. "We can't prove it yet, and we might be wrong." She went to the whiteboard beside Jones, took the marker from her, and scrawled "Suspect" under "Victim" beneath William O'Connell's picture.

Vic arrived only a few seconds behind his commanding officer. All four of them stared at the whiteboard for thirty seconds or so.

"It fits," Vic said at last. "Maybe."

"We'll have to ask Skip," Erin said. "But I'll bet the scene would look about the same if O'Connell died setting a bomb as if he died trying to disarm it."

"And we need to check the wife's finances," Jones said. "I'm on it." She swung her chair around and went to work at her computer.

Webb snapped his fingers. "Okay, great," he said. "O'Reilly, you should talk to Mrs. O'Connell. You connected with her better than the rest of us when we were there. You good for that?"

"Sure thing, sir."

"I'll talk to the bomb squad," Webb said. "I'll get confirmation about the scene. Jesus, we should've seen this before. The toolbox, the mob connections... This is fantastic."

Only Vic didn't seem keyed up. He was staring at the whiteboard, a scowl on his face.

Erin shouldered up beside him. "What's the matter?" she said.

"It's not enough," he muttered.

"What, you want to beat up some more Irish guys before we're done?" she said.

"Yeah, whatever," he said absently. "Something doesn't

quite fly here."

"You think we're wrong?"

Vic didn't turn to look at her. He kept drilling holes in the board with his eyes. "No, I don't," he said. "But I think we're missing something. Why a car bomb? There's gotta be ways of offing his wife that wouldn't attract so much attention. He had a gun, for God's sake. He could've shot her right in the face."

"Neshenko," Webb said. "If the guy was a criminal mastermind, d'you really think he would've blown himself apart with his own bomb? Come on. Nineteen times out of twenty, it really is this simple."

"Okay, I'll go to see Mrs. O'Connell," Erin said.

"Call me when you're done," Webb said.

"Yeah," Jones said from behind her computer monitor. "And come straight home, young lady."

Vic snorted. "I'll stay here, go over the files again."

"While you're at it, draw up a search warrant," Webb said. "We'll need to go through the O'Connell residence again, look for bomb supplies."

"Don't forget to call for backup if the lady throws down on you," Jones added.

"I've got my backup right here," Erin said. "Rolf, *komm!*" The Shepherd sprang to his feet and trotted out of the office at her side.

*   *   *

When Erin buzzed the O'Connell apartment and identified herself, Cynthia paused so long that Erin thought she might have to head back to the precinct for that search warrant. But then the lobby door clicked open.

Cynthia met her at the door to the apartment, but stood in the doorway, leaving Erin and Rolf in the hall. "Detective," she said, "I really am quite busy at present, and I cannot imagine what you have to say that was not covered at our last encounter."

"Ma'am, I just have a few questions about the case," Erin replied. "If I could come in for a few moments?"

"Must you bring that horrid animal with you?"

Rolf stared up at the woman with cool contempt.

"Ma'am, he's a well-trained police dog," Erin said. "He didn't damage anything the last time he was here. He'll be right beside me the whole time."

Cynthia sighed. "Very well, if you must," she said, stepping to one side.

Erin was surprised to see how much the apartment had changed. At least half the clutter had been removed, and most of the rest stood in open packing boxes. "Are you in the process of moving, Mrs. O'Connell?" she asked.

"No indeed," Cynthia said. "I am simply divesting myself of unwanted encumbrances."

Erin blinked. "I see."

"These useless bric-a-brac belonged to William," Cynthia explained. "They have neither sentimental nor aesthetic value. However, they have some monetary worth, and shall serve to defray the expenses brought upon me by his passing."

"Fair enough," Erin said.

"Now that we have sufficient room, I can offer you a seat," Cynthia said. "Please."

"Rolf, *sitz*," Erin commanded as she sat at one end of the living-room couch. Rolf took up his place beside the arm of the couch.

"Now then," Cynthia said, seating herself on a straight-backed hardwood chair and clasping her hands in her lap. "What were your questions?"

"I understand there were some economic difficulties you

and William were experiencing," Erin said. "And I know there was a small life-insurance policy for William."

Cynthia bristled. "If you are suggesting that I had anything to do with his death—" she began indignantly.

"No, ma'am," Erin said. "I wanted to know whether there was a similar policy for you."

Cynthia stopped short. She cocked her head at Erin, very much like an inquisitive bird. "Why ever would you ask such a thing?"

Erin thought of what Carlyle had said. "Bombs aren't particular about who they kill," she said. "I need to know whether anyone would benefit economically from the death of either William... or you."

"There is a policy in my name," Cynthia said. "But I still don't see—"

"Ma'am, you had a meeting of your garden club on the morning of the bombing," Erin said. "Did your husband need the car for anything before that meeting?"

"No."

"Then why was he in the garage?"

"You would have to ask him," Cynthia said sharply. "He certainly did not bother to inform me of all his movements."

"Ma'am, who are the beneficiaries of your life insurance?"

"My sister, and William, of course."

"And what is the value of the policy?"

"Three hundred thousand dollars."

Erin nodded. "How does that break down between William and your sister?"

"William would have gotten two-thirds of it, while Edna would receive the remainder."

"So you get twenty grand from William, but he would have gotten two hundred thousand if something had happened to you?"

Cynthia gave Erin a long, level stare. "That would seem a reasonable approximation of our relative value, yes."

Ouch, Erin thought but didn't say.

Then it hit the other woman. Cynthia's eyes narrowed as she made the connection. "Detective, you surely do not mean to say that my husband was seeking to kill *me*."

Erin kept quiet, letting her think it over.

"But," Cynthia said, and for the first time, her composure cracked. "But... he would never... I mean, *really*. The whole thing is too absurd."

"Is it?" Erin asked, staring at Cynthia's face.

What she saw made her feel ashamed of herself. She didn't mind breaking crooks in interrogation. It was satisfying to reduce a street thug to a quivering blob. But this woman wasn't a criminal. Cynthia was snooty and arrogant, but now she was figuring out that her husband, a man she'd despised as a good-for-nothing gambler, might have been trying to murder her. He'd very nearly succeeded, too.

Cynthia slumped back in her chair, looking suddenly ten years older. "This is simply too awful," she said.

"Ma'am, does your husband have a workshop or something?" Erin asked. She had to ask it a second time before the other woman looked up from her private thoughts.

"No, no, we have no room to spare here," she said.

Erin's mind raced. William had probably assembled the bomb on location. If it hadn't been done in the apartment, maybe he'd done it somewhere else in the building. "Ma'am, do you have any clothing William wore recently?"

"I laundered all his used clothing," she said.

"What about a shoe?"

Cynthia stirred herself from the chair. "Yes, I have his shoes in a box to go to Goodwill," she said, going to the front entryway and returning with cardboard box. "What do you need with a shoe?"

Erin had also stood up. "I want to trace William's movements," she explained. "If I could borrow this for a few minutes?"

"Keep it, for all I care," Cynthia said. "Used footwear has no intrinsic value." She was recovering herself a little, but still looked pale. It was clearly a shock to realize how close she'd come to being blown to bits.

Erin took the black leather shoe and held it to Rolf's nose. "Rolf, *such*," she ordered. She went to the apartment door and opened it.

It took the Shepherd a moment or two to orient himself. This was the scent of a man who'd lived in the apartment, who'd come and gone through the door daily. Rolf needed to sort out the freshest scent, and he was uncertain. But he trotted gamely off to the elevator.

Erin cursed to herself. They'd have to try every level for a positive result, since there was no way to know which floor, or floors, William had exited on. At least it wasn't a very tall building. She started with the basement.

They were lucky. Rolf leapt enthusiastically out into the parking garage and, nose glued to the ground, tail waving, launched himself into his hunt. Erin was pleased, but not too surprised, to note that he didn't go straight toward the explosion site. He went instead to a door marked MAINTENANCE. Then he stopped short and sat, staring at the door.

Erin was momentarily puzzled. If he was following his normal search drill, he was supposed to scratch at the base of the door. His sitting response was an alert to his other training.

She froze. William's shoe dropped from her hand unnoticed, bouncing away from her feet. Police dogs were trained to sit in response to smelling explosives.

Erin yanked out her phone and speed-dialed Webb.

"That was quick," the Lieutenant said. "Did you find—"

"Are you still talking to Skip?" Erin interrupted.

"Well, yes," Webb said. "But—"

She cut him off again. "I need him down at the crime scene," she said. "Rolf tracked O'Connell to a maintenance room, and there may be another bomb inside."

"We'll be right there," Webb said, all business. "Don't touch *anything*."

"Copy that."

Chapter 11

Erin was pretty sure the maintenance room wasn't booby-trapped. She was impatient to see what was inside. But she also wasn't stupid. When there were bombs in the area, it was always a good idea to wait for the professionals. She gave Rolf his ball to reward him for his tracking and alert, then spent a few minutes watching him. Her partner enjoyed his paycheck more than any other cop she knew. The big, fierce German Shepherd turned into a puppy again, gnawing energetically at the rubber chew-toy and ignoring the outside world.

It seemed like a very long time, but the bomb squad's van rolled into the garage just a few minutes later. Skip was driving, Webb riding shotgun with him. A couple of other bomb techs dismounted from the back, lugging bags of gear.

"Hey, Erin," Skip said. "What've we got?"

"Rolf alerted to this door," she said, pointing. "He tracked O'Connell here, then told me there were explosives on the other side."

"Okay," Skip said, cracking his knuckles. "Let's have a look. Erin, you and Lieutenant Webb please stand back. I want you against that wall over there." He indicated the wall shared by the maintenance door, about twenty yards away. "Just a precaution."

Erin obeyed, knowing they would just be in the way if they hung around. The detectives watched the bomb guys do their thing.

One of the other techs brought Skip a flexible fiber-optic line. He got down flat on his stomach and fed it slowly under the door, where there was a gap of about half an inch. The other tech had set up a laptop and was seated against the wall. He controlled the cable remotely, scanning the inside of the room.

"No ambient light," he said. "Switching to IR. I've got a space about eight by ten, some shelves on the right, boxes on them, a tool rack on the left. The door looks clean. No wires, no devices attached. Nothing free-standing in the room. Concrete floor, clean and dry. Got one light bulb in the middle of the ceiling, pull-rope switch."

Skip pulled the fiber-optic back out and handed it to the first tech. "I think we're good. I'll pop the door. Brent, take a few steps back."

"You want to put the suit on?" Brent asked.

"Hell no," Skip said. "You hear me say how small that place is? I won't be able to move with that damn thing on. If whatever's in there goes up, I don't give a damn about open-casket."

"A lot of EOD guys say the only thing a bomb suit is good for is keeping your corpse pretty if a bomb goes off in your face," Webb explained to Erin.

She swallowed. That wasn't a very reassuring thought.

Skip didn't seem concerned. He gently twisted the doorknob. "Locked, of course," he said.

"I'll get the super," Webb said. The building superintendent had let them in but had remained outside the garage, only too happy to stay away. One bomb had already gone off in his garage, and he had no interest in being near another. The Lieutenant returned in a few minutes, absent the super, but holding the man's keys. He gave them to Skip with a wry smile.

Skip got the right key on the second try. Everyone had gone completely silent. The click of the lock was very loud. He slowly pushed the door open, being careful to keep hold of the knob and not letting it swing freely. With his other hand he drew out a big D-cell flashlight. Erin figured he wouldn't risk using the light switch.

"Whew," he said. "I can smell the nitro. Someone's been getting funky with the chemicals in here. No wonder your dog freaked. I'm gonna go slow and easy. Brent, I'll hand you stuff as I clear it. Don't drop anything."

"Nitroglycerin goes off if you drop it, doesn't it?" Erin asked quietly.

Webb nodded. His face was tight and tense. "Don't worry, it's not likely they'll find much. Any explosion will be pretty small and local."

"That's not gonna do Skip much good," she muttered.

Several nervous minutes passed as the bomb-techs worked the scene, carefully clearing stuff out of the closet. Their movements were almost slow-motion. They announced every action to one another as they did it.

Skip thrust his head out of the room. "Okay, Erin, Lieutenant, you can come over now. We're good."

Not entirely trusting him, they approached. "Rolf, *bleib*," Erin ordered. Rolf stayed with his ball, happy enough to keep chewing away.

It was a tight fit with the two detectives and the bomb technician crammed into the room with the shelves, though most of the stuff on them had been moved out into the garage. Skip played his flashlight over a cardboard box on the second shelf from the bottom.

"That's it," Skip said. "Nitro."

Erin crouched down, peering into the box without touching it. "Is it safe?" she asked.

"Pretty much," he said. "It degrades over time, becoming unstable, but this stuff's basically brand-new. But it's an undiluted contact explosive, so if we drop this box on the floor, it'll probably go off and blow all three of us apart."

She stood up again and took a respectful step back.

"How much is there?" Webb asked.

"Not a lot," Skip said. "I'll have to weigh it. But I've got four canisters here. Two of them are acid, nitric and sulfuric, chemist supply labels on them. Then there's glycerol here. The fourth can's got the finished product, but I think it's just leftovers from the main bomb. We found a tub and a couple gallons of bottled water, a measuring cup, and some paint-stirring sticks."

"How's this work?" Webb asked.

"You mix the acid and glycerol, one part each," Skip explained. "That makes the nitro. It's pretty simple stuff. The problem is, it's temperature-sensitive, and the mixing process produces heat. So you have to use the water as coolant. If the mix gets above thirty degrees C, you can get a runaway reaction. That sends out nitrogen dioxide gas, which is poisonous, of course, and there's a high chance of spontaneous detonation."

"Jesus," Webb said, and from the look on his face, Erin could tell he was thinking about the possibilities of a mad bomber working with such unstable stuff in the basement of a building full of people.

"Yeah," Skip agreed. "I hope the guy who did this didn't have a clue what he was doing."

"You *hope* that?" Erin demanded. "Why?"

"Because if he knew what he was doing, he's out of his goddamn mind," Skip said. "Working with it at all is dangerous, but in a confined space with no ventilation? It's almost as bad as cooking meth. He's lucky he didn't kill himself with this shit."

Webb and Erin glanced at each other. "We think maybe he did," Erin said.

"Oh," Skip said, getting it. "That figures."

"Taylor, given what's here, and what you observed from the blast site, can you tell us if there's any nitroglycerin missing?" Webb asked.

"I think this is all of it," Skip said. "And there's other supplies here. There's a metal saw, some steel powder that'll probably match the bomb casing. I think the whole thing was manufactured right here. This is a bomb lab, ladies and gentlemen, but it only made the one bomb as far as I can tell."

"Thank God for that," Webb said.

"Amen," Skip and Erin said in unison.

"Okay, we're going to need this stuff packed up as evidence," Webb said.

"Yeah, sir, that's not gonna happen," Skip said.

"What do you mean?"

"I'm not taking homemade nitro into the precinct," Skip said. "I'll take a very small sample to test at the lab, make sure it's the same stuff from the explosion. Then we're taking the rest of this out of town and detonating it. Unless you'd rather fill out the incident report when the lab blows up. Because I'll be in no condition to do paperwork."

"Right, of course," Webb said, a little abashed. "Okay, let's get some pictures, and collect your samples. I assume the rest of the stuff is fine to keep as evidence?"

"Sure," Skip said. "The acid's only dangerous if you get it on your skin, or huff the fumes."

"Can we dust for prints?" Erin asked.

"Yeah, if you're careful," Skip said. "If you're going to pick up that can, give me a thirty-second head start."

"Is this one of those things where if we see the bomb guy

running, we're supposed to try to catch up?" she asked.

"Pretty much."

"Okay, Detective," Webb said to her. "We'll dust for prints, then get the nitroglycerin out of here and collect the rest of the evidence. But I think we know what we're going to find. We get O'Connell's prints off the bomb supplies, we've got our case closed. Attempted murder resulting in death from an accidental detonation of a destructive device. Plus insurance fraud, just to pad out the file."

"Yes, sir," Erin said.

She went through the usual crime-scene procedures. She felt a strange letdown. She'd cracked the case, but there wasn't the usual rush of triumph from bringing in the perp. She'd gotten more satisfaction from busting Frankie Fingers and his two goons. Maybe it was the fact that the guy they were locking down for the bombing was on a slab in the precinct morgue. She couldn't very well slap the cuffs on him.

Erin shook her head and buckled down to work. Being a detective wasn't working out quite like she'd imagined.

*   *   *

One thing was always the same, Erin thought. Patrol cops, detectives, all of them were slaves to paperwork. Forms and reports ate up the entire rest of the day. Getting an early start at the O'Connell apartment just meant she was able to go home on time instead of having to stay late. By the time the squad powered down their computers and turned off the lights, they were bored and tired.

As Erin clipped on Rolf's leash and got ready to go, Webb walked over. He extended his hand.

"Congratulations, Detective," he said. "You've got your first major case closure."

She took the offered hand. "Thanks," she said. "But..."

"But what?" Webb said.

"Did we do any good, sir?"

He looked confused. "What do you mean?"

"There wasn't going to be another bombing," she said. "And it's not like the guy got away with it. So what was the point?"

"Detective, this job's got all the meaning you put into it, and that's it," Webb said, and in his eyes Erin saw only the faintest flicker of the young, idealistic cop he'd been twenty years ago. "You start looking for anything more, you're going to burn out faster than a cigarette."

"I'll keep that in mind, Lieutenant."

"Good work, O'Reilly. I mean it," he said. "Your dog, too. Give him a steak, or whatever. And I'll see you tomorrow. There's eight million more crimes waiting to happen."

*   *   *

Erin and Rolf trotted down the stairs, ready to be done with the day. They passed the duty officer's desk without looking at the man behind it.

"Erin?" he called, sounding surprised. She skidded to a stop and turned to face him.

"Malcolm?" she exclaimed, almost as surprised as he was.

He grinned. "I thought it was you!" he said. "Didn't know you were up in the big city. How's your dad these days?"

Brendan Malcolm was one of Sean O'Reilly's former colleagues, another Irish cop from the old neighborhood. Erin had seen him often while she was growing up, her dad and the other cop working the same areas in Queens. He was a burly man with a thick mustache. The mustache was grayer, and his waistline had gained a couple inches since she'd last seen him, but he was the same guy she remembered.

"He's good," she said. "Just talked to him."

"Enjoying his retirement?"

She laughed. "He always said he wanted to live on a lake, with fish in the water and deer in the woods, and now he's got it. He's pretty happy. What about you? I thought you'd have hit full pension by now."

"I got my twenty a while ago," he said. "But I haven't found anything I like doing better. So what're you doing up from Queens, and out of uniform?"

"I'm not working Patrol anymore," she said. "I made detective, just transferred up here."

Malcolm whistled. "And here I was thinking you were just out of the Academy. Where the hell does the time go?"

"Into the pension fund," she said.

Malcolm laughed. "Damn right. So you're part of Holliday's new unit?"

"Yeah, under Webb."

"What're you working?"

"Bomb case," she said. "Just closed it. Guy tried to take out his wife, blew himself up instead."

"Nice," Malcolm said. "We don't get many bombs. It's not like back in the old country, thank God."

"Funny you should say that," Erin said.

"How come?" He scratched his cheek. "Wait a second. You don't mean it's an Irish guy did it?"

"Afraid so."

"You know why they call it a paddy wagon, don't you?"

"I always thought it was because of Irish cops."

Malcolm shook his head. "Maybe, maybe not. No one's sure whether it's a nickname for the guys riding up front, or the guys riding in back."

She had to smile. "What was it like, back when you were my age?" she asked.

"Oh, back then?" He grinned. "Well, for starters, we didn't have all these fancy toys. We didn't have cell phones, Internet, color TV..."

"Electricity, indoor plumbing..." Erin broke in.

"Okay, it wasn't *that* long ago," he said. "What do you want to know?"

"Were there a lot of Irish perps you had to bring in?"

"Well, yeah," he said. "You remember our neighborhood, Erin. Half the names were O'Something, and the other half were McWhatever."

"I mean, did you ever feel funny, having to take in a guy with the same background? Did you ever think, there but for the grace of God?"

Malcolm rubbed his mustache, becoming more serious. "You talking about the Irish mob? You know, that's an old nickname for the NYPD, too."

"That's exactly what I mean," she said.

"I guess it's like being a black cop in Harlem," he said. "But then, there's Chinese cops in Shanghai, aren't there? What do you think they do when they bust a guy? Say, 'Hey, you're Chinese, so am I, just run on home and we'll call it a day?'"

"I guess not," Erin admitted. "Did you ever have any run-ins with the O'Malleys?"

"You talking about Evan O'Malley's crew?"

She nodded.

"Yeah, they were up-and-coming in the '90s," he said. "Started really street-level, like they always do, so we had a few brushes. Protection rackets, dealing contraband. There was one guy, I forget his name, made a bundle smuggling cigarettes over the Jersey line. 'Course, I was just working Patrol, so I didn't know what was going on higher up. Your dad would be the guy to ask about this. He got involved with the garbage-truck thing back then."

"Yeah, I know," she said. "He told me about that." She leaned in over the desk, lowering her voice. "C'mon, Malcolm, you've gotta have a story about these guys. Spill."

"Okay," he said. "I do have one Irish story. This is, oh, ninety-five, I think. My partner and I get a call to this bar, not too far from La Guardia, place called MacKenzie's. There's been a brawl. We roll up, go in, the fun's all over. Nobody fighting anymore. There's this one guy lying on the floor by the bar, head just busted to pieces, blood like you wouldn't believe. We take one look, I know we're calling the ME, no point in a bus. I've got a few years in, I've seen some shit, my partner's this wet-behind-the-ears Academy pup, he takes one look and stumbles outside looking for some sidewalk to paint. I'm standing there, I ask who called it in. Nobody saw nothin'. They all just look past me, like they're staring at someone standing in the doorway over my shoulder. I say, well, clearly there's been a crime committed here. Someone want to tell me what happened?"

Malcolm shook his head. "At last, the bartender says, with an Ulster accent you could cut with a knife, 'Well, copper, the poor lad took a tumble, must have hit his head.' I look at the floor, I look back at the barkeep, and I point to the bar stool next to the body. It's busted to pieces too, there's one leg of it torn off, and there's blood all over it. It's cracked, splinters hanging off it. This is the most obvious murder weapon I've ever seen, okay? And the barkeep says, 'Oh, I think he might've hit that on the way down, broke it to bits.'"

"Are you shitting me?"

"God's honest truth," Malcolm said. "It gets better. I'm thinking like you are. I say to the guy, 'Bullshit.' He says, maybe catches something in my voice, 'What's your name, lad?' I say, 'It's *Officer* Malcolm.' He looks me over and says, 'And are you from Ireland, Officer Malcolm?' I tell him it's none of his damn business, but yeah, my folks came over back in the day. He shakes his head and says, 'Lad, this is Irish business. It's the Troubles, and needn't concern us here. Let it be.'"

"*Let it be?*" Erin exclaimed. "It's a *murder!*"

"I know," Malcolm said. "But what can I do? This whole bar's full of guys thinking like him. Here I am, my partner's losing his supper outside the front door, I can't get a statement that's worth the paper in my summons book, and I'm just a patrolman. I punt, call in for the Homicide dicks, and once they get there, I hand it off to them."

"You ever find out what happened?" she asked, fascinated.

"Nope," he said. "We never even found out who called us. We did get an ID on the vic, though. Guy named Art Doyle, Northern Irish national. Not a nice guy; these days, Homeland Security wouldn't even let a guy like him in. I followed the case a little, found out he was probably with the UVF. That's the Ulster Volunteer Force. A bunch of paramilitary thugs, kind of the Protestant version of the IRA. If anything, worse. They were a terrorist organization, as bad as Al Qaeda. Mostly killed Catholic civilians."

"Jesus," Erin said. "So do you think the IRA whacked him?"

"I doubt it," Malcolm said. "A hitman's not exactly going to beat a guy to death with his own bar stool, is he? But I think you're partway right, all the same. Someone with Irish Republic sympathies might've recognized him, or heard him say the wrong thing, and took it badly. Then the others covered for him."

Erin shook her head, unable to think of anything to say.

"So here's the thing, Erin," Malcolm said. He reached across the desk and laid a hand on her shoulder. "It's not about being an Irish cop versus an Irish criminal. Our old country's torn in half, and here we're no different. Those guys in the bar, they didn't trust a cop, not even an Irish one. And why should they? Where they came from, if someone got taken out, you either quietly applauded it, or you got even yourself, in your own good time. And those are the guys who came over here and built the Irish mob. They're tough, and they like to solve their own problems." He smiled. "Glad you closed the case. But I've been talking at you long enough. You've had a long day, and I'm making it longer."

"It's fine, Malcolm," she said. "I appreciate it. Guess I'll see you around."

"Until I retire," he said.

"Or until I do," she shot back. "I swear, they're gonna have to pry your shield out of your cold dead fingers."

"Maybe so," he agreed. "You take it easy, Detective O'Reilly."

Chapter 12

One piece of excellent news was that among the endless forms had been Erin's application for a take-home vehicle. Normally this would have taken a few days to process, but K-9 cops got special consideration, since their specialized vehicles were by far the best way to transport the animals.

Distracted by the novelty of driving home, and thinking about her conversation with Sergeant Malcolm, Erin was halfway there before the thought struck her that she should be celebrating. But it was too late to turn around and invite any of her squad-mates out for drinks, and she didn't feel right calling up any of her old buddies from Queens. She wasn't dating anyone at the moment, either. She glanced in the rearview mirror at Rolf's compartment. He was staring out the window, putting noseprints on the glass.

"Guess it's just you and me, hey, partner?" she said. The dog, attuned to her attention, perked his ears and looked at her.

When she arrived at her apartment, she decided to take Rolf for a long walk through the neighborhood. Whatever Webb said, Rolf wasn't the sort of dog who got food as a reward. He wasn't a Labrador getting fat off table scraps. He was a working dog, bred for intense drive and focus. His reward for doing good work was to play with his toy, or to get another job to do. The best thing she could do for him was to get him outside after the long afternoon of report-writing and let him run off his energy.

It felt good to her, too. The evening was cool enough to be comfortable, the air clear. They ranged through their old haunts, walking their beat together, moving at a brisk walk. By the time they got back to the apartment, Rolf's tongue was hanging out and he was glad to settle in for a rest.

Erin decided to go out. She could really use a drink, and didn't want to do it at home. The best way to become an alcoholic, her dad had warned her, was to drink alone. And Rolf didn't count. She put his food out for him, gave him a good rub behind the ears, and went down to the Priest, her local bar.

It was middle evening and the bar was crowded. She slipped through the gathered drinkers and caught the bartender's eye.

"Hey, Nate," she said, raising a finger.

"Evening, Erin," he said. "What can I get for you?"

Oh, what the hell, she thought. "Irish car bomb."

He raised an eyebrow. "Careful where you order that, girl."

"Are we in Belfast, Nate? Pour the damn drink."

"Coming right up," he said. He slapped a glass on the bar and began pouring Guinness. "What whiskey?"

"Do you have Glen D?" she asked, remembering the signature label of the Barley Corner.

"Don't know it," Nate said.

"Make it Jameson, then."

"Now there's a fine drink to be having," said an unmistakable Irish brogue from just to her right.

Erin spun around to look straight into the smiling, sparkle-eyed face of James Corcoran. "What are you doing here?" The words came out without her thinking about them. She winced inwardly at her lack of tact, but his smile didn't falter.

"Oh, I'm on a date, love," he said.

She glanced past him. "Really? Where is she?"

"I'm talking to her."

Erin couldn't help smiling. "Do you use that line on every woman you meet in a bar?"

"Only the ones it's true about."

Nate placed a glass of Guinness on the bar and got ready to drop the bomb shot into it.

"That one's on me," Corky said, flicking a finger upright. "And I'll have one for myself."

"Thanks," she said.

The bartender got out the ingredients for another car bomb and handed the shot glasses to Erin and Corky. Corky poised his shot glass over his Guinness. "Shall we, love?"

Erin dropped her bomb in unison with him. The two of them drained the powerful concoctions together. The glasses clanked down to the bar simultaneously.

Corky shook his head briskly and blinked. "Not bad!" he said.

Erin felt the whiskey burn in her throat and swallowed a cough. A car bomb was one of the quickest ways to get drunk she knew, and she already felt lightheaded, but her cop instincts were still tingling. "Have you been following me?" she asked.

"Perish the thought," Corky said. "I told you what I was doing at our last meeting. I'm not following you. That would be creepy and downright undignified. I'm pursuing you."

"What's the difference?"

"Well, for starters, you have to know you're being pursued. And I did warn you."

"Okay," Erin said, leaning an elbow on the bar and facing him directly. "Now I know. What else?"

"When a lad's only following someone, he may not be attempting to catch her," Corky explained. "I'm certainly looking to catch up to you."

"And then what?" she asked. "Now that I'm here, and you're here."

"Well, I'd have thought that was obvious," he said. "Or have I been unclear in my intentions?"

She snorted. "You don't waste much time, do you?"

"It's been my experience that we've no guarantee of any extra time to be walking this earth," Corky said, and for just an instant his face grew more serious. Then his smile came out again. "Why be wasting what we've got?"

"Mr. Corcoran," she began.

"Please, love, Corky." As he said it, he laid a hand on the back of her own hand, where it rested on the bar.

"I'm not that kind of girl," she said, but she liked the feel of his fingers and didn't move her hand. He had a surprisingly gentle touch, and his confidence was compelling. She found herself wondering how those skillful fingers would feel touching her somewhere more personal, and hoped the thought wasn't showing in her face. What was the matter with her? It must be the strong drink.

His forehead crinkled. "Fair enough, love," he said, still smiling. "I'll not be wanting anything from you that you're not willing to give. I'm not that kind of a lad."

"What kind of lad are you?" she asked. "I don't know anything about you, except that you're Irish and you like to hit on women in bars."

"And what is it you're wanting to know? Should I be having my lawyer about me?"

Suspicion skated across her consciousness. That was the trouble of being a cop. She couldn't just turn it off at the end of a shift. He was making a joke, that was all. She laughed. "Corky, this is a conversation, not an interrogation. A lot of guys can't shut up about themselves. Go on, tell me something about you."

He grinned. "Half a moment, love." He signaled the bartender. "Whiskey for me, straight up, and bring this fine lady whatever happens to be her pleasure."

Erin realized his hand was still resting on hers. She wondered why it didn't bother her. "Guinness," she said, wanting to keep at least some of her wits about her. If she kept hitting the hard stuff, she'd end up on the floor.

"Now then," Corky said. "As you've no doubt guessed, I was born in Occupied Ireland, Belfast to be precise."

"Occupied?"

"By the British, of course," he said. "They claim it's part of their United bloody Kingdom, but we fine Irish lads dispute the matter. I was raised Catholic, altar-boy in fact."

"I wouldn't have taken you for a religious man," she admitted.

"I'm not, particularly," he said. "But you've got to believe in something. And you?"

"I'm Catholic, yeah," she said. "Raised in the church."

"I'd think police work was the sort of thing to diminish a lass's faith," he said.

"I guess you've got a choice," she replied. "We see people at their absolute worst, on the worst days of their lives. That makes some of us a little cynical. But I figure, that's exactly the sort of things that make faith important."

"Good soldier of Saint Michael, is that it?" he asked, naming the patron saint of police officers.

"Pretty much," she said. "And what do you do, Corky?"

"Oh, I'm in the shipping business," he said. "Moving things from one place to another. You'd be surprised how much money's in it."

"What kind of shipping?" The suspicion flared up again.

"I work with the Teamsters, negotiating contracts with companies." He grinned. "They say I've a way with people. I can be right persuasive."

"Is this where you tell me how rich you are?" She sipped her Guinness.

He winked. "Only if you like your men to be wealthy." Then he laughed. "I do well enough. I'll admit I probably make more than your detective's salary."

"That's not saying much."

"Something I've wondered," he said. "Don't the higher-ups in your organization worry that paying their coppers so little is an incentive to corruption?"

"My dad says it keeps the guys who want to make money in the private sector," Erin said. "It leaves police work to folks who aren't trying to get rich, but want to make a difference."

"So your old man was a copper, too?" Corky asked. "He must be right proud of you."

"I hope so."

"And what about the rest of your family?" he asked. "How many O'Reillys are there, and what do they do with themselves?"

"I've got three brothers," she said. "Two older, one younger. Sean's a trauma surgeon, Michael's in business. Tommy's... Tommy."

"What manner of business does Michael do?"

"Commodities trading."

"Grain futures and the like?"

"I think so," she said. "Every time Mike tries to explain what he does, I fall asleep."

He laughed. "You're a lass who likes the action, I take it. No, I don't think I can see you nine-to-five, riding a desk."

"You, neither," she said.

He laughed again. "Fair to say. I like to keep on the move."

"What brought you over from Ireland?" She finished off her glass of stout and set the empty glass back on the counter.

"Ah, this is America, land of opportunity, didn't you know? They've a grand statue they set out to welcome me and everything. It's the old immigrant story, same thing that brought your grandparents over, I'll warrant."

"I see," she said. "What about your family?"

"What about them?" His mouth still wore its smile, but his eyes were suddenly wary. His hand tightened on hers ever so slightly.

Erin hesitated. "Sorry. Didn't mean to pry. If it's something you'd rather not talk about..."

"There was a saying in my old neighborhood," Corky said. "Everyone always said, there wasn't a Corcoran who ever amounted to anything. I may be the best of a bad lot." Then he recovered. "So I came here to make something of myself, where I'd have the chance to do it."

"So what else do you do, besides work and buy drinks for women?"

He winked again. "I don't mind saying, I'm a right fine dancer. If you're not too worn out from a day of chasing criminals, would you care to step out on the floor with me?"

"I shouldn't," she said. "I've got work tomorrow."

"So have I," he said. "What's that to do with anything?"

The hell with it, Erin decided. "Okay, why not."

"Grand!" Corky exclaimed. "The night's young. Not to worry, I'll have you home before your old man starts to worry."

"My old man's retired and living upstate," she said. "I haven't worried about him waiting up for me since high school prom."

"You'll have to tell me that story."

"Some other time," she laughed. "Once the statute of limitations runs out."

She slid off the barstool. As she stood up, disengaging her hand from Corky's, her elbow hooked her empty beer glass toward her. It skidded over the edge of the bar between them.

Corky's hand shot out, snatching the glass out of midair before it was halfway to the floor. He set it back on the bar.

Her mouth hung open. She'd hardly seen his hand move.

"Reflexes, love," he said with a shrug and a smile. "I've always been good with my hands. Perhaps I can show you some other tricks."

"Is everything about you fast?" she asked.

"I can take my time," he said, looking her straight in the eye. "When it's called for."

Erin was glad she didn't blush easily. "You talk a good game. Let's see what you've got on the dance floor. You know any good clubs?"

"I think you know this neighborhood better than I do," Corky said. "I'll be delighted to take you wherever you want to go."

Outside, in the parking lot, he pointed. "There's my ride."

"You've got to be kidding me," she said. "Isn't that a little... much?"

Corky's car was a BMW convertible, bright yellow and spotlessly clean.

"I'm fond of autos," he said. "As I told you, I like to keep moving."

"Do I even want to know how many times you get pulled over in that thing?"

He opened the passenger door for her. "Less than you'd think, love. Usually I outrun the coppers."

"I can bust you from inside the car, you know," she said.

"Handcuffs and everything?" Corky inquired as he got into the driver's seat. "And there you were, telling me you weren't that kind of girl." He started the engine. It caught with a deep, throaty growl. "Now, where are we going?"

Chapter 13

Erin directed Corky down 278 over the border into Brooklyn, to a dance club called Bembe. It was small, and even on a weeknight the place was crowded. A line had formed outside, the beat of the music calling to them from halfway down the block. "Can you salsa?" she asked him.

"Love, I can dance any step you care to request," he said.

"This place is cash only," she said suddenly, remembering. "They've got an ATM outside if—"

He grinned and patted his pocket. "Not to worry, love."

When they made their way inside, the air was hot and close from warm, fast-moving bodies. The customers were every shape, size, and color. A DJ with impressive dreadlocks clamped under his headphones had two fingers thrust into the air, eyes closed, moving with the music.

Erin paused, with a cop's reflexes, scanning the crowd for potential threats. But Corky took her hand and pulled her forward with that smooth speed she'd seen earlier that evening. He moved with the easy grace of a cat, loose-limbed and suave, and Erin thought he might be the most physically attractive man she'd ever met. Not that he was covered with muscles or sporting movie-star good looks, but his charisma was making her almost dizzy.

She reminded herself to take it easy. She'd only just met the guy. Her dad had told her that men never respected women who went to bed on a first date. But as they started to dance, moving in rhythm to the hot Latin beat, she found herself wondering how his skin would feel under her hands, how his lips would taste, whether he'd be smooth and cool or fierce and passionate, and...

He drew her in close, and their bodies were suddenly pressed tight against one another. His green eyes sparkled as he looked into her own, and she knew he could read, or guess, most of what she was thinking.

The song ended, to cheers from most of the crowd. Erin licked her lips and stepped back. "I need a drink," she said.

"Aye, it's bloody hot in here," he agreed. A thin film of sweat was on his forehead, but he didn't seem to be out of breath. If anything, he was more relaxed than before.

They went to the bar and ordered rum punch. Corky pronounced it a little weak, but acceptable, and finished his quickly. Erin savored hers, taking smaller sips, and leaned on the bar.

"So, love, what are we celebrating?" he asked.

"Do we need a reason?"

"Simply being out with a fine lass such as yourself is reason enough," he said. "But I've a hunch there's something more."

She nodded. "I closed my first case with Major Crimes."

His eyebrows shot up. "Really? That's grand! What manner of miscreant did you haul off to jail?"

"I didn't get the chance," she said. She wondered what she ought to tell him, but this would all be in all the papers tomorrow anyway, so there couldn't be any harm. "A guy tried to blow up his wife, but screwed it up and took himself out instead. I helped prove it was him."

Corky laughed. "Ah, it takes a bit of the sweetness out of victory, finding out the lad was already done for, doesn't it?"

"Yeah. I'll say," Erin said ruefully. "Vic thinks there's something more to it, and I guess I do too. I need to think—"

"Ah, love, you're much prettier when you're smiling," he said. "Take those wrinkles out of your forehead. They'll make you old before your time."

She smiled. "Anyway, I guess they'll keep me as a detective. I always thought I could do it, but you've gotta find out for yourself, you know?"

"I know exactly what you mean," he said with a wink. "You can hear as much as you want about it, but until you do it for yourself, there's no way to know quite what it's like."

Erin gave him a look. "I was talking about police work."

"Of course you were," he said, his face innocent as the altar boy he claimed to have been.

"Enough of this," she said, finishing the last of her punch and pushing away from the bar. "We came here to dance."

They danced until exhaustion brought them to a standstill. Corky was right. He seemed to know every dance step known to man, as well as a few he made up on the spot. As they moved together, Erin realized what was so damned attractive about him. He was such a physical being, a man of action. Erin was the same way. So, she thought, was Rolf. No wonder she made such a good K-9 officer.

But the other thing that made her a good officer was discipline. So when his hands started wandering in their dance, she moved them back to safe territory, even though a part of her—a large part—wanted to let him go where he wanted. He accepted the corrections with good humor. In fact, there was a look in his eye that suggested he liked the chase as well as the capture. With that in mind, she let herself get a little flirty, even suggestive.

At last, though, she knew it was time to call it a night. It was well after ten, and they were a good half hour's drive from her apartment. "I don't know about you," she said, having to lean in close to be heard over the music and background noise, "but I've got to get up in the morning."

"More dead criminals to discover?"

She laughed. "Not all of them are dead."

"I should hope not! I'd not want you to be deprived of the thrill of pursuit."

"Are you all right to drive?" she asked. It had been over an hour since either of them had had a drink, but Corky had knocked back two strong rum punches, as well as the car bomb and whiskey earlier.

"Never better, love," he said. "But perhaps you'd like to take the controls?"

"Really?" She'd wanted to, but hadn't dared ask. Erin liked fast, powerful cars; yet another perk of being a cop.

He handed her the keys as they walked out of the club. "Just don't get us pulled over."

"Are you kidding?" she retorted. "Once we cross into Queens, that's my old beat. I'll know all the guys on the road."

"But just think of their feelings," he said. "They'll see you with me, and their poor hearts will be broken."

She rolled her eyes. "I never date cops," she said, opening the door of the convertible. Corky didn't bother with his door, sliding over the top of it and into the passenger seat.

"Why's that?"

"It's not a good idea to mix work and romance," she said. "Policing is still a guy's world. It's hard not to be a sex object when you're a woman on the force. Bring actual sex into it and... it's trouble."

"I see what you mean," Corky said. "Fortunately, I'm no

copper."

Erin gave him a quick smile as she started the car, feeling the thrum of the engine through her feet. She took a moment to adjust the mirrors and get a feel for the vehicle, then put it in gear.

Corky leaned in close, brushing a loose strand of hair back from her neck. Her skin tingled at the near-ticklish touch. Then she jumped as his lips pressed softly against her neck, just behind her ear. The cool night air raised goosebumps on her arms as her perspiration cooled, but his breath was warm.

She kept driving, looking straight ahead. He kissed her neck again, then slid a hand up to touch the side of her face, caressing her cheek.

"I'm driving!" she exclaimed, as he turned all the way toward her in the seat and slipped his other hand onto her leg, just above the knee. "You want to cause an accident?"

"Ah, you've plenty of self-control," he said. "I've no doubt you can handle the situation."

"You're just lucky I left my Taser at work," she said.

"So you're saying you want sparks to be flying between us?"

"Have you ever been tased?" she countered. "It's not a pleasant experience."

"Aye, I have."

"Really? What for?"

"Disorderly conduct. I was somewhat the worse for drink at the time. It was all a tragic misunderstanding."

"What did you think of it?"

"I asked if the officers wouldn't mind giving me a second helping."

Erin took her eyes off the road for a second. "You didn't."

"Aye, I did," he said, his face showing nothing but earnest truth.

"And did they?"

"Aye, they gave me another jolt, for the crime of gross stupidity."

"Did you ask for a third?"

"Nay, I didn't want to be greedy."

Erin shook her head. She'd had to submit to a Taser jolt when she'd been issued her own to carry, and one had been more than enough. "You're something else, Corky."

*   *   *

She pulled into her apartment's lot, parking in a visitor space. Leaving the engine running, she unbuckled her seatbelt and turned to face him.

"Thanks," she said. "This was fun."

"Are you sure you want me to be leaving?" he asked.

"I need to get some sleep," she said. "Gotta be sharp tomorrow."

He unfastened his own belt. "That wasn't an answer," he said, and then he had his arms around her and his lips tasted of just a hint of rum, and she closed her eyes and let the kiss unfold. And she arched her back into him without fully realizing what she was doing. Oh, she wanted him.

But she couldn't. Not yet, not tonight.

He felt the change in her, the way she gently disengaged. He pulled back a little, so they were eye to eye. "Are you sure?" he asked again. "This could be something wonderful."

She managed a shaky smile. "No kidding," she said. "But that's not the point." She sat up and redid her ponytail. Even though they were both fully clothed, she felt disheveled, half-naked.

He smiled, and the smile warmed her right to her toes and made her question her decision. "Well, love, if that's your way of thinking, I'm bound to respect it," he said. But the way he looked at her had much more to do with desire than respect.

"Jesus," she muttered, half to herself. "You're the guy my dad warned me about. You know, the one every dad tells his daughter about when she starts noticing boys."

Corky threw back his head and laughed. "I'm one of them," he agreed. "But I doubt I've ever personally met your old man."

Erin got out of the car. Corky climbed out of his seat and came around to the driver's side. They stood facing each other, close together.

"Just because I'm not saying yes tonight," she said, "doesn't mean I'm saying no forever."

"I know it," he said.

"Goodnight, Corky."

"Goodnight, Erin."

They moved toward each other in unspoken unison. She took his head in her hands. They kissed, letting the moment linger. Finally, they stepped reluctantly apart.

"Shall I call you?" he asked.

"You don't have my number."

"Of course I do," he said. "Nine-one-one, aye?"

She laughed. "You do know there's over thirty thousand cops in New York, right?" She thought about it. "I may end up working some strange hours," she said. "Why don't you give me your number, and I'll call you?"

"Grand," he said, and rattled off the digits. Erin logged the number in her phone.

"Well, see you around," she said.

"Aye."

Erin went into the apartment, still feeling a tingle in her lips and a heat inside her that had nothing to do with rum punch.

Chapter 14

Erin didn't sleep well, despite her fatigue. There were way too many things going on for her to let go of them. She dozed off, then snapped awake, then drifted for a while, then woke up again.

She gave it up at four in the morning. The sun wouldn't be showing for a while yet, but she got out of bed anyway and put on her running clothes. Rolf, who'd slept much better than his partner, was instantly on his feet, excited at the prospect of an early-morning run.

She jogged through the dark streets, unconcerned about muggers. At four o'clock most of them were sleeping off their drug of choice, and the ninety-pound German Shepherd at her side was a pretty effective deterrent. She hoped that by working her body she could quiet her brain.

Little flashes of clarity moved through her thoughts like the glow from the streetlights as she passed under them. But the overall picture stayed dark. When she got back to her apartment at five-thirty, she'd broken a good sweat but was no closer to figuring out what was bothering her.

There was only one thing to do. After putting on the coffee

and grabbing a quick shower, Erin did what every good cop did when faced with trouble. She called for backup.

*   *   *

A lot of retirees wouldn't have answered the phone before six AM. But Sean O'Reilly, Senior, had always been an early-morning riser. He'd bought the house in upstate New York when he'd left the NYPD so he could go right out on the lake, or into the woods, depending on the fishing or hunting season. He picked up the phone before the third ring, sounding wide-awake.

"O'Reilly," he said, having never quite broken himself of his old patrolman's style of answering.

"Hey, Dad."

"Erin! Everything okay?" He was instantly alert and concerned.

"Yeah, Dad, I'm fine," she said. "Sorry it's so early."

"It's okay. I'm on the kitchen phone. Your mother's still in bed. I was getting set to take the boat out, see what's biting."

"You got a minute?"

"I've always got time for my favorite daughter. What's on your mind?"

"I'm your only daughter." She took a deep breath and sorted through her thoughts. "I got my first Major Crimes closure."

"Really? Great work!" Sean exclaimed. "What can you tell me?"

"I told you a little the last time we talked. There was this guy who got in deep with some bookies. He was a collector for one of them, working off the debt, and tried to make a big score by offing his wife for the insurance."

"Classic. You get him?"

"Not exactly. He screwed up setting a bomb in her car and

blew himself up."

"He was the car bomb guy?"

"Yeah. So he's our man, but he's already dead. So... we got it closed, but..."

"Not very satisfying?"

"Right," she said. "And I don't know, it's..."

"Not what you figured it'd be?" he suggested.

"Maybe that's it," she admitted. "But..."

"But what?" he said. "Kiddo, what's eating you? Are you sure he's the guy?"

"Yeah. Well, I mean... I'm pretty sure."

"Is it the Carlyle thing?" Sean asked. "Look, Erin, that was years ago. Did he get inside your head on this?"

"No! Well, maybe a little. But there's Irish mob fingerprints all over this."

"Do you mean actual fingerprints, or..."

She smiled. "No, Dad. I mean, this is the sort of thing they'd do, right? I mean, car bombs aren't common over here. But there's this guy who was with the IRA, building bombs for them, and another suspect fingers him for us, and it turns out he had nothing to do with it? Does that sound right to you?"

"You had a suspect give you Cars's name? Can you tell me who?"

"Just another Irish thug," she said. "Young guy. I don't think you'd know him."

"Another Irish guy sold out Carlyle?" Her dad sounded skeptical. "Did he volunteer the info, or did you lean on him?"

"We leaned pretty hard," she said. "But look, Dad, we're sure O'Connell killed himself. The blast pattern, the tools he had out... hell, we found his bomb lab in the basement! It wasn't Carlyle."

Sean O'Reilly was quiet a few moments. "Then what's the problem?" he finally asked.

"There's gotta be more to it."

"Why?"

"Why a car bomb? There's a hundred easier ways to kill someone. Safer ways."

"If this guy knew Carlyle, he might've had car bombs on the brain."

Erin nodded. "Yeah, that makes sense. But why'd the other guys try to feed Carlyle to us?"

"I've seen some of the Irish mob in action," her dad said. "These guys aren't rats. Code of silence, y'know? They're not gonna sell out another of theirs, not if they're buddies."

"What if they weren't buddies?"

"They still wouldn't bring the cops into it," he said. "The Harbor Patrol would be scooping a body out of the East River."

"Then why would they tell me Carlyle did it?" she wondered aloud.

"You'd have to ask Carlyle that," Sean said dryly. "Or the guy you talked to."

"I think maybe I'd better," she agreed. "Guess the case isn't quite closed yet."

"Guess not," her dad said. "But remember, Erin, you won't always know everything. You're not gonna get all the answers every time. If you know who, and why, that'll have to be good enough. Otherwise you're not gonna be happy as a detective."

"Right, Dad," she said. "Look, I have to get to work. Say hi to Mom for me, okay?"

"You can say it to her yourself," Sean said. "She just came into the kitchen. Mary, why aren't you asleep?"

Erin missed most of her mother's answer, but then her mom's voice came on the line, loud and clear.

"Erin, how are you?"

"Fine, Mom, but I need to get going here."

"All right, dear. But you really should come up here to see us soon. We miss you, honey."

"Sure thing, Mom. I miss you too. Especially your pie." Mary O'Reilly's baking had been well-known in their neighborhood while Erin was growing up.

"I'll bake whatever you'd like best," Mary said. "And if you have a nice young man you can bring with you, I'll feed him too."

"Mom!"

"Come on, dear, isn't there somebody...?"

"Mom!" she said again, but she knew her voice had given her away. "Okay, there is a guy I just met, but it hasn't really gone anywhere yet. We're not at the meet-the-parents point."

"Is he a good Catholic boy?"

She rolled her eyes. "Yes, Mother, he's a Catholic. He's a former altar-boy from Ireland. I'm sure you'd like him. But I really need to go now. Traffic into Manhattan's gonna be a killer."

"All right, dear. But at least tell me your young man's name."

"James. Goodbye, Mom."

"Lovely. Well, have a good day at work, dear. I love you."

"Love you too, Mom, Dad. 'Bye."

* * *

When Erin got to the Major Crimes office, her first thought was that the place had been burglarized. File folders were strewn on the floor, arrest reports, mug shots, crime-scene photos, all jumbled together. A small wall of cardboard boxes from Evidence had been constructed around Vic's desk. The big Russian sat in the middle of it all, eyes bloodshot, the largest soda cup she'd ever seen at his elbow.

"Jesus Christ, Vic," she said. "Have you even been home?"

"Huh?" He looked up. "What time is it?"

"Quarter to eight," she said, then added, "in the morning."

"Shit," Vic said. He cleared his throat and said it again. "Shit."

"So what's all this?" she asked, gesturing at the snowstorm of paperwork.

"Irish mob," he said. "All the known associates of Carlyle, O'Connell, Fergus, the rest of them. There's gotta be a hundred of these guys. You have any idea how many Irish crooks there are in the five boroughs?"

"Almost as many as there are Irish cops," she said with a smile. "Find anything?"

"Not really," he admitted. "Carlyle's the only one with a history of bomb-building."

"So someone was trying to set him up," she said. "O'Connell was making it look like Carlyle bombed him."

"Because of the gambling debts? Yeah, I thought of that," Vic said. He took a slurp of whatever was in the cup on his desk. "So maybe he was trying to frame Carlyle. So what? He's still dead, so what's it matter?"

"It matters if someone put him up to it," she said. "That makes it conspiracy. If anyone helped him plan it, that makes it Murder One on whoever helped."

"That's gonna be impossible to prove," Vic said. "Whoever it is, he'll just say they never discussed it, and that's it. Dead end, unless someone was enough of a moron to record the conversation. Believe it, Erin. I've been beating my head on this all night."

"Okay," she said. "Well, who are we looking at? We can at least narrow the list down a little."

"Let's see," Vic said. "Carlyle works for Evan O'Malley. Evan's an old-school mob boss, real big on loyalty. From what I hear, he wants you dead, you'll know it was him. A frame isn't his style. Then there's the rest of the O'Malley lieutenants. There's Mickey Connor, he's chief enforcer, bombing's not his

style, though. More of a face-to-face guy. Frankie Fingers, of
course, we know already. Liam McIntyre, he's a possible. Don't
know much about him. We think he's big into narcotics. Then
we've got James Corcoran, smuggling; Veronica Blackburn, runs
whores..."

"What?" Erin's throat felt suddenly thick and swollen, her
hands cold.

Vic looked at her quizzically. "Veronica Blackburn," he
repeated. "Runs whores. I don't see what—"

"No, the other one," Erin said. "The smuggler."

Vic rummaged through the files on his desk. "James
Corcoran," he said. "Here he is. Another Irish import. Same
neighborhood as Carlyle. File says they're best friends, grew up
together. You know the guy?"

Erin took the file, willing her fingers to stay steady. The
mug shot was unmistakable. Corky was even smiling slightly
into the camera, that mischievous sparkle in his eyes. "No," she
said quietly, "I don't think I do."

"I don't know that I like him for this," Vic said. "Childhood
friends? I can't see them coming apart like this. Unless we're
missing something."

Erin barely heard him. It took all her willpower not to
crumple the photo in her hand and scream at the ceiling. She
took a deep breath, held it, let it out again. "You're probably
right," she said, and was glad to hear that her voice sounded
more or less calm. "He doesn't look that subtle to me."

"Read the file," Vic said. "He's a cocky son of a bitch, that
one. They say he never carries a gun. Got a guy says he just
keeps a knife on him. And the bastard's fast enough he can get
away with bringing a knife to a gunfight."

"Yeah," Erin said absently, remembering how Corky had
caught the beer glass she'd knocked off the counter. "But does
he know about bombs?"

"He could. He and Carlyle were in the IRA together."

"I think," Erin said, still speaking quietly, "someone needs to have a talk with Corcoran."

"Maybe," Vic said, but he sounded dubious. "I think we need to remember how we got pointed at Carlyle."

"The bomb," Erin said. Then she managed to shake her head clear of her personal feelings for a few moments and think like a cop again. "And Fergus's guys. They sold him out to us."

"Yeah," Vic said. "I thought the Lieutenant cracked them, but..."

"They played us," Erin said. "Damn it, that whole scene in the interrogation room was scripted!"

"We wouldn't have believed it if they'd given it up easy," Vic said. He was on his feet now, excited, pacing back and forth.

"They knew we'd be coming, once we figured out O'Connell's connection to Fergus," Erin said.

"I don't think their plan included getting their asses kicked," Vic said.

She shrugged. "Maybe they're smarter than we thought."

"That wouldn't take much," Vic said. He was walking faster, working his hands into fists, then shaking them loose again, over and over. "Okay. Let's try this for size. Frankie hates Carlyle. Why?"

"He's jealous," Erin offered. "Carlyle's a bigger guy in the organization, especially in the sports book."

"Okay, he wants Carlyle's book," Vic agreed. "So why not just whack Carlyle?"

"Cars is too strong to go after directly," she suggested. "He's well-connected, maybe O'Malley wouldn't sanction the hit."

Vic snapped his fingers. "Yeah! But what if Carlyle took out someone else and got caught doing it? That leaves Frankie clean."

"I dunno," Erin said. "It seems awful complicated. Maybe

Fergus found out O'Connell wanted his wife dead and just grabbed the opportunity."

"Okay, sure," Vic said. "Why not? O'Connell's working for Fergus, he comes up to him one day, says, 'Hey, boss, I got this wife, she hates me, but there's an insurance policy. It'd pay off my debts, you think we could make this work?'"

"Fergus suggests using a car bomb," Erin said. "Makes it look like his rival did it."

"Two birds, one stone," Vic said.

They stopped, staring at each other. "It's Fergus," they said in unison.

Then Erin sighed. "So what? We can't prove it. The bomb was built on-site. Fergus never would've touched it."

Vic shared the sigh. "It's down to he-said, she-said, and O'Connell's not exactly gonna say anything. But we've got it! We just need to hold on, and something's gonna shake loose." He grabbed his cup off his desk and took another long pull on the straw.

"Vic? What exactly are you drinking?"

"Mountain Dew," he said. "Might be some caffeine pills crushed up in it. Sixty-four ounces."

She blinked. "And they say the Irish have a drinking problem. Your kidneys are gonna kill you."

"Better than my liver," Vic said. "I could've put vodka in it."

"Well," Erin said, thinking out loud, "if O'Connell talked to one guy about murdering his wife, he might've talked to others first."

"Could be," Vic said. "You want to brace some of the Irish?"

"Oh, I'm definitely going to be talking to at least one of these guys," Erin said, gritting her teeth. "But I'm thinking we take one more crack at Fergus's boys. Try them when they're not on a script."

"I wouldn't mind having a few minutes with those two

goons," Vic said. His hands clenched again. "Sometime they're not looking to take a dive."

"You and me both," she said. At that moment, Erin really wanted to hit something.

A shout echoed from the stairwell.

"What in the name of God is going on?"

Erin and Vic looked up, instinctively guilty, to see the face of Lieutenant Webb. He waved his hands at the mess in disbelief.

"What the hell have you done to this office?"

"Redoing the filing, sir," Vic said. "O'Reilly was helping me."

Webb looked from one of them to the other.

"Had to be done, sir," Erin said, fighting down a sudden, hysterical laugh. "Otherwise we couldn't find anything."

"Okay, I can't deal with this," Webb said. "Not before my coffee. By the time I'm done with my second cup, I want to be able to see the floor."

"On it, sir," she said.

"And on the subject of paperwork," Webb went on, "I want the reports from the bomb lab on my desk before noon."

Vic stifled a groan. He and Erin got down on their hands and knees, to the great interest of Rolf, and started bundling the files back into their boxes.

*   *   *

The cleanup didn't take as long as Erin thought it might, but the final result promised to be a little confusing the next time anyone tried to research the O'Malleys. Jones arrived partway through and lent a hand. Rolf lay beside Erin's desk and supervised.

"Okay," Webb said. "That's better. You know we can't leave crap lying around like that. Next thing you know, we'll have

Chinese takeout and empty pizza boxes everywhere."

"Like I found my desk," Erin said. "Sir?"

"Yeah?"

"Vic… Detective Neshenko and I, we were thinking we should talk to Fergus one more time."

Webb glanced at the two of them. "Really? What for?"

"We think he helped O'Connell plan the bombing."

The Lieutenant rubbed his chin. "You think that, do you?"

Vic and Erin nodded.

"Any particular reason?"

Erin went to the whiteboard and started writing a list, talking as she did it. "O'Connell worked for Fergus. They had a lot of chances to discuss this. O'Connell was connected to the Irish mob, through Fergus again. Fergus has motive to want Carlyle out of the picture, but probably doesn't want to cause an internal war. Fergus and his buddies tossed Carlyle under the bus when we leaned on them."

"Okay," Webb said. "I can see how all that could fit together. But detective work isn't about building a plausible story. It's about building a case. And for a case, you need evidence. Do you have any?"

"Nope," Vic said. He didn't seem troubled by the fact.

"And your plan to get this evidence is…?" Webb prompted.

"We're gonna ask," Vic said. He paused, then went on, "nicely."

"You know I can't get you a search warrant on this."

"What about the dog?" Vic asked.

"What about him?" Erin echoed.

"Can't he get us a warrant?"

"No," Erin said. "I can take Rolf along, and he'll alert if he smells explosives. If Fergus was speeding and we stopped his car, that'd be enough for us to search it. But to go into his house? The dog's not enough for PC."

Webb shrugged. "She's right," he said. "Do you really want to be the poster children for the next Supreme Court civil-liberty case?"

"Maybe we can spook him," Erin said.

"How so?" Webb asked.

"I'll reintroduce him to Rolf," she said. "See what happens."

"O'Reilly," Webb said, "be careful. No lawsuits. Follow the rules—all of you."

"Sir, he's not gonna bite him," she said. "Not this time."

Chapter 15

As Erin and Vic went down the stairs, Jones fell in step with them.

"Want to get out of the office, see how the real cops work?" Vic asked.

"I dunno," Jones said. "You see any real cops around?"

"So," Vic said to Erin. "What's the plan?"

"We shake Fergus, see what falls off him."

"How?" Jones asked.

"If he's guilty, he'll make some assumptions," Erin said. "That may make him react."

"Okay," Jones said, but she didn't look convinced.

They took two cars to Bernie's, Erin and Rolf in her Charger, Jones and Vic in Jones's Taurus. It was a little before eleven o'clock, not exactly peak time for a bar. Erin did a drive-by, but couldn't see anything through the smudged glass of the front window. They parked around the corner and consulted.

"Vests?" Vic suggested.

"Vests," Erin agreed. "This could get ugly."

They strapped on their body armor, including Rolf's K-9 vest. Whenever the dog wore his armor, he knew it was time to do serious work. His tail whipped back and forth, his nose twitching. Vic went into the trunk of his car and came up with a Remington 870 pump shotgun. Erin checked her Glock, Jones her Sig-Sauer.

"Okay," Vic said. "Someone needs to watch the back, in case any of them do a rabbit. Erin's up front, we'll need the dog, and damned if I'm sitting this out, so that leaves you, Kira."

"Fine with me," Jones said.

"You hear us call, you come in hard," Vic said. "Otherwise, stay in the alley." He looked Erin over. "You've got the lead on this, as long as we're talking. But if shit goes tactical, I'm calling the shots."

Erin didn't argue. She was trying to control the pounding of her heart. It was silly. They'd been in here before, with no real problem. But now they were deliberately provoking trouble. She wondered if they should have more backup. But they weren't serving a warrant. This was still a fishing expedition.

"Right, then," Vic said. "Ready when you are."

Erin took a deep breath, patted the grip of her Glock in its holster, and twitched Rolf's leash. "*Fuss,*" she said, ordering him to heel. The Shepherd went into motion, sticking to her side in perfect step.

The interior of the bar looked exactly like they'd left it. The broken glass from their previous fight had been swept into a corner, but no one had even bothered to pick it up. The place was deserted except for Damien Knox, still wearing the marks of the beating Erin had given him. He looked up, blinked, and his mouth dropped open.

"Hey, Damien," Erin said with a sweet smile. "Remember me?"

"What the hell you want?"

"Just coming in, taking a look around," she said. Vic drifted to the side, splitting off from her and taking up a covering position. His shotgun was held easily, angled so it was pointing toward the floor but in Knox's general direction.

"You got a warrant?" Knox demanded.

Erin didn't have a warrant. But she didn't need one yet. They were in a place of business, and a cop had just as much right as anyone else to walk in the door. If there was something obviously illegal going on, or an illegal substance in plain view, like a pile of cocaine on the bar, they could take action. But they couldn't search the place. And they certainly couldn't go upstairs, to the apartment where Fergus was probably hanging out, at least not without permission. She wondered if Knox knew all this, deciding he probably did. Few people were better versed in search-and-seizure law than career criminals.

But he might not know so much about police dogs. It was time to run her bluff. "You know what I've got here?" she asked. "This is Rolf. He's a K-9 police dog."

"No shit, lady," Knox said. He was trying to keep an eye on her, Rolf, and Vic all at once, with the result that his eyes were darting back and forth. He was backing slowly away from them.

"He's a trained detection dog," she went on. "That means he can find explosives. It doesn't matter if they're hidden. And if he tells me there's a bomb in here, I can search the whole place." That wasn't completely true. Generally speaking, a dog giving a positive alert only counted as reasonable suspicion, not probable cause. There were exceptions, mostly pertaining to potential acts of terrorism, but that got complicated.

"So what?" Knox retorted, but he licked his lips as he said it and his eyes kept darting. Erin saw the fear in his eyes, and knew she'd guessed right.

"Frankie didn't build the bomb for Fourth-Place Billy," she said. "But he knows how. And he's got another one here, doesn't he. Rolf, *such!*"

Rolf started sniffing, head down, tail whipping side to side.

Knox hesitated. Then he made his decision. Erin saw the look that came into his eyes an instant before he acted. *Oh, shit,* she thought. Then things happened very fast.

Knox reached behind the bar in a quick motion. Erin was moving, too, and out of the corner of her eye she saw Vic bring up his Remington.

"Don't!" Vic shouted.

"Rolf, *fass!*" Erin snapped simultaneously, ordering him to bite and releasing the catch on his collar. She went for her gun.

Rolf gave a ferocious snarl and sprang at Knox.

Knox's hand came up with a sawed-off double-barreled shotgun. The hammers were already cocked and ready. He swung the weapon to cover the charging dog.

Erin had the Glock in her hand, but she felt like she was moving through deep water. "Drop it!" she and Vic yelled with a single voice. But she already knew he wasn't going to.

Vic had been the only one of the three with a gun already in his hand, and it gave him a split-second edge. The Remington roared, the sound overlapping the double blast of the sawed-off.

Vic's shot caught Knox in the right shoulder, spinning him clean around. It deflected the other man's aim as he fired. The sawed-off had an impressive spread, though, and pellets sprayed into the dog, along with just about everything in the front half of the bar. Rolf staggered sideways, losing his forward momentum. Erin felt something smack into her chest and something else brush past her cheek with a rush of air. She didn't care. She hardly even noticed. She had her Glock in line, sighting down the barrel at the man who'd just shot her partner.

In some corner of her brain she knew that he'd fired both barrels of the sawed-off. The weapon was empty. In that instant, though her instincts screamed at her, and the law would be on her side, she decided not to kill him.

As she hesitated for that brief moment, Rolf scrambled back

into forward motion. The thing about K-9s was that they didn't know how to lose. In their training, they always, always won. Getting hit only made them mad. If you were going to shoot at a charging K-9, Erin knew, you got only one shot at it, and God help you if you didn't put the dog down with that shot.

Erin didn't have a clear line of fire anymore, as ninety pounds of extremely angry dog hit Knox, smashed him against the bar, and brought him down, teeth clamped on his gun-arm.

Vic pumped another shell into his shotgun and scanned the room, weapon held tight to his shoulder. Erin rushed Knox. "Drop the gun!" she shouted, but between Knox's screaming and Rolf's growling, she might as well have been yelling baseball scores.

It didn't matter. The shotgun fell out of Knox's hand. He flailed at Rolf's head with his free hand, which did him no good at all. Rolf kept up a continuous growl and tightened his grip.

Erin kicked the sawed-off away from the scuffle. Knox's blows were getting weaker and he was clearly out of the fight. She reached to the back of her belt with her left hand and pulled out her cuffs. She glanced at Rolf and saw blood flecking his cheek where a shotgun pellet had grazed him, but he didn't seem otherwise injured. His vest had stopped most of the blast.

Vic had his phone out. "Ten-thirteen, shots fired!" he barked into it. That was sure to bring every cop within a ten-block radius. They'd have all the backup they needed, Erin thought, just in time for the fight to be over.

The door to the upstairs apartment flew open. It was the exact wrong moment. Vic had only one hand on his shotgun, his head bent to talk into the phone. Erin was fumbling with her handcuffs, her Glock pointing down at Knox's face. Rolf's teeth were fully engaged in biting Knox.

Erin acted on reflex, bringing up the Glock. Another guy was coming through the doorway. Even as she saw the revolver in the man's hand, she snapped off a one-handed shot. He sagged back against the doorframe, blood blossoming on the thigh of his jeans. She'd clipped him with her lucky shot. She dropped the cuffs to get both hands back on her pistol and went into a shooter's stance. "NYPD! Drop it or I drop you!"

The man dropped the gun, a nickel-plated .38, and clapped his hands over the leg.

"Let it bleed! Hands in the air!" Vic shouted.

Erin recognized Gary Morgan. "Who else is upstairs?" she demanded, closing the distance.

"Help..." Knox whimpered from the floor. No one paid him any attention except Rolf, who wasn't interested in helping him.

Morgan muttered something inaudible.

The moment these two meatheads had started shooting at cops, the rulebook had changed. They could search everything and detain everybody in the place. "Where's Frankie?" Erin shouted in Morgan's face.

He was going pale from shock, even though the wound didn't look too serious. He sank to his knees, his hands in the air. "Upstairs," he said.

Vic grabbed Morgan and slung him around, cuffing him with brutal efficiency. He booted the revolver into a corner. "Go!" he barked at Erin. Sirens were sounding in the distance, closing fast.

"Rolf! *Pust!*" she ordered. The dog released his victim and trotted to Erin's side. His tongue was hanging out. At least someone was enjoying this, she thought. He didn't seem to have noticed the wound to his face, and he was still very eager for action. "*Voran!*" she said, giving him the command for a blind search of a building. This was a risky order. He'd bite anyone he found inside. But it was a pretty good bet that the only guy in the place was Franklin Fergus, and he could well be waiting with a gun at the top of the stairs. Procedure in this situation called for sending the dog in first.

Rolf went up the stairs at a run, Erin close behind him. Vic kept an eye on the two wounded men in the bar. As Erin climbed the stairs, she heard the rattling scrape of a window being opened.

Rolf disappeared around the corner in the upstairs hall. He growled, Frankie Fingers screamed, and then there was a loud thud from outside, followed by Jones's voice yelling, "NYPD! Don't move!"

Erin rushed after her dog into a bedroom. The window hung wide open. Rolf was on his hind legs, forepaws braced on the windowsill, looking down and wagging his tail. Peering out the window, she saw Frankie Fingers in the alley below, spreadeagled face-down on the pavement and clad only in leopard-spotted boxer shorts. Jones stood over him, gun in hand.

"Jesus!" Jones called up to Erin. "What'd you do to this poor guy? He went out the window like a damn flying squirrel! Lucky he didn't break his neck."

"Good boy, Rolf," Erin said, scratching him behind the ears. "Good boy." But their job wasn't quite done. "Cuff him!" she called to Jones. "We've got two creeps wounded inside. Backup's inbound."

They had to clear the rest of the apartment. They did it more carefully now, moving room to room. They found nothing until they came to the spare bedroom. The moment they stepped inside, Rolf froze, then sat in his alert position. Erin recognized the stuff at once. Nitric acid, hydrochloric acid, glycerol.

"Son of a bitch," she said. It was another bomb lab.

*   *   *

The sirens were louder, right outside the bar now. Doors

slammed and men shouted. Backup had arrived. She didn't pay much attention. Her focus was on her partner. She dropped to one knee in front of him, running her hands carefully up his legs, checking for broken bones or open wounds. Rolf quivered with excitement, his whole body rigid, but he didn't seem to have any serious injuries. Three balls of buckshot had slammed into his vest, but the Kevlar and ceramic plate had stopped them from doing real damage. She checked his face, seeing a shallow laceration over his eye where Knox had punched him and the buckshot wound on his face, between his eye and his jowl. A single piece of shot had lodged there. Blood trickled down the dog's face.

"Erin! You hurt?" Vic appeared in the doorway. Behind the big Russian was a pair of uniforms, guns drawn.

"Huh?" She looked over her shoulder at him. "No, I don't think so."

"You caught one," Vic said. "I saw it. Stay right there." He came into the room, laying his shotgun on the floor and kneeling next to her.

"I'm fine," she said. "Rolf got tagged. I've gotta take care of him."

"Of course we'll take care of him," Vic said. "But we're taking care of you, too." He looked her over. "Damn, girl. Lucky break." He pointed to her chest.

Erin looked down at herself and saw a pellet of metal lodged in her vest, center mass. She remembered the blow she'd felt when Knox had fired his sawed-off. "Holy shit," she said. Her knees felt suddenly weak, even though she knew perfectly well she wasn't hurt. The realization that she'd been shot was overwhelming, now that the fight was over. She sank back, sitting on the floor.

"Hey, it's okay," Vic said. "You're gonna be fine."

"I know," she said. "It didn't penetrate."

"I see that. But it might've cracked a rib. Can you breathe okay?"

"Sure."

Vic grinned at her. "First gunfight?"

"I've been shot at a couple times," she said. "Never hit before."

"How's it feel?"

"I could use a drink."

He threw back his head and laughed. "Not till after they take the blood test, make sure you're not hopped up." He looked around the room then. "Jesus. Another bomb?"

"Maybe. We'd better get Frankie into an interrogation room, see what he's got to say about it."

Vic glanced out the window. Jones had their man against the alley wall, cuffed. "Please tell me we're gonna put some pants on him first," he said. "How come every time we arrest this guy, I gotta see what color his boxers are?"

*   *   *

Things slowed down again, which was fine with Erin. It gave her a chance to recover a little. Cops swarmed all over the building. The CSI guys showed up to collect spent brass and dig bullets out of walls and woodwork. Paramedics picked up Knox and Morgan, both of whom were bleeding all over the place. One of the medics took a look at Rolf, plucked the lead pellet out of his cheek, and pronounced him good to go. Then the CSI guys wanted to collect blood samples. Vic and Erin had to hand over their guns and fill syringes, along with giving their statements.

It was almost two hours before they were finally able to get back to the precinct. Jones had booked Fergus and had him in the interrogation room. Webb was waiting for them in Major

Crimes, hands on his hips.

"Neshenko," he said quietly. There was a hard edge to his voice.

"Yes, sir," Vic said, coming to attention.

"Is this your idea of asking nicely?"

"Yes, sir," Vic said again.

Webb stared at the ceiling, as if he was looking for divine inspiration. "I send you to ask some questions, and now I've got two bodies in the hospital, shots fired, and it's a miracle no one's in the morgue. Please just tell me no cops got hurt."

"Rolf took some buckshot in the face," Erin said. "He'll be fine."

Rolf, blood crusting his cheek, managed to look both unconcerned and tough at the same time.

"Okay," Webb sighed. "I've got Fergus in Interrogation Room One, but it won't do us much good. He seems to have forgotten how to say anything but 'lawyer.'"

"So where's that leave us?" Erin asked.

"It leaves you and Neshenko on modified assignment, until we get the shooting cleared."

"It was righteous," Vic protested. "They had guns in their goddamn hands! What were we supposed to do? Erin got shot! Of course we put them down. And they're still alive, aren't they?"

"That's enough, Detective!" Webb snapped. Vic blinked and fell abruptly silent. "Do you really think it's no big deal for the NYPD to pop off rounds in Manhattan? We are going to do this by the book. You and O'Reilly are going to keep your heads down, keep quiet, and do as you're told." His voice softened a little. "You okay, Detective?" he asked Erin.

"Fine, sir," she said. "Vest caught it. I'm not even bleeding."

"You know, we've got people you can talk to after an incident like this."

Erin's temper flared. "Yeah," she said sharply. "If I faint, I'll know where to go."

"You're keyed up," Webb said, "so I'll give you a pass on that one. But it's time both of you shut up and get back to work. If I'm not mistaken, you've just earned yourselves a hell of a lot of reports to fill out."

Feeling a little like naughty schoolchildren, Vic and Erin went to their desks. Webb wasn't kidding. There were arrest reports, Use of Force reports, reports about reports, an endless pile of paperwork. They were also required to debrief in response to the Critical Incident. This meant sitting down with Doc Evans, the departmental psychologist.

Erin didn't want to talk about what had happened. She wanted to keep moving, to get out of the precinct and back on the street. She knew she was still loaded with adrenaline and the emotions of the fight, but that didn't change how she was feeling. She managed to schedule the debriefing for later that afternoon, at four o'clock. By the time she'd waded through the first wave of paperwork, it was a little before two. Webb was talking to Fergus and his lawyer down in the interrogation room. The other members of the squad were at their desks. The silence was oppressive.

She stood up. "I've gotta get out of here," she said to the room at large. "I need to clear my head, stretch my legs."

"Modified assignment," Jones reminded her. "Besides, we don't have any more perps to chase down."

"I know that," Erin said. "Is it okay if I go out for a while? I'll be back in time for my hand-holding session at four."

"As long as you wear your mittens, look both ways at street corners, and don't talk to strangers," Vic said.

Jones reached into her desk drawer. "Nice smart mouth you got there," she said. "I'm gonna come over and staple it shut, see how funny you are then."

Erin clipped on Rolf's leash and left the building. She knew she was being silly, but she couldn't stand the thought of the whole afternoon cooped up with the anger that was still bubbling in her. Some of it was aimed at Fergus and his stupid goons. She knew she'd escaped getting killed by pure luck, and so had her partner. But she'd dealt with the bad guys. She wasn't sorry she'd fired at Morgan now; she was sorry she hadn't fired a couple more times and put him down hard. That was the wrong way to feel, and she knew that too, but she couldn't help it.

Most of all, though, she was angry at Corky and at herself.

It wasn't a smart thing to do, but Erin wasn't interested in doing the smart thing. She loaded Rolf into the Charger and drove to the Barley Corner.

Chapter 16

It was two-fifteen when Erin parked at the Corner. She felt a momentary doubt at going in without her sidearm, but that was how modified assignment worked; until she and Vic were cleared with respect to their gunfight, she wouldn't get her piece back. But she brushed the thought away. This wasn't going to be a shootout. She was looking for just one guy, a guy who didn't carry a gun by all accounts. And she had Rolf to back her up. Besides, as mad as she was, maybe it made sense not to have a firearm on her.

She marched straight in the front door and glared around the room, her partner standing stiff-legged beside her. The place was nearly empty. The lunch rush was over, and the after-work crowd hadn't shown up yet. Danny, the bartender, was there, as was a waitress, a handful of guys at the bar, Morton Carlyle in his place of honor at the end of the bar, and James Corcoran holding forth at a table with three of his friends.

Corky was in the middle of a funny story. He was on his feet, working up to a punchline. "So the lass says, 'Corky, what's my mum going to say?' And I say, 'Love, your mum *was* the other girl!'"

Sharing the laughter of the other guys, he looked over and saw Erin. A smile of recognition, its warmth charming in spite of everything, lit up his face. "Erin, love! Fancy seeing you here!"

"Corcoran," she growled. "I've been looking for you. You son of a bitch."

He blinked, his smile faltering. Then he recovered. "Love, whatever you're thinking I've done, I assure you—"

"I'm not your love, damn it!"

Carlyle was on his feet, coming in from her left, his hands spread in a conciliating gesture. "Miss O'Reilly, is something the matter?"

"You keep out of this!" she snapped at him.

He didn't flinch. "I'm not directly involved in this matter," he said, "but this is my establishment, and I don't appreciate my customers being harassed."

"What about your close friends?" she demanded.

"Them, either," he replied coolly.

"Ah," Corky said. "So that's the problem, is it?"

"Look, Corks," one of his friends said, rising to his feet. "Whoever this chick is—"

"Detective O'Reilly, NYPD," she said. "Get your ass out of here before I kick it clean down to Brooklyn."

Corky's buddies glanced at one another, then at Carlyle. The Corner's proprietor nodded to them.

"Go on, lads, give us a moment," he said. "I'm sure this is something we can sort out in a congenial manner."

They hesitated. He snapped his fingers and pointed to the door. They got up and left, abandoning half-finished drinks. That left only the three of them, Danny the bartender, the waitress, and four guys at the bar. All the others ignored the altercation.

"All right then, Miss O'Reilly," Carlyle said. "We've a few quiet moments. Have you something to say to my associate here?"

"God damn it," she said, furious with him for being so calm, for trying to mediate, for existing in the first place. "You're always so helpful. Always trying to do a good turn for the cops. Never want anything in return, do you? No way. You just store up favors like a bank account, waiting for that rainy day. Yeah, I talked to my dad about you. He spent half his career waiting for you to call in that favor. Thought that was pretty funny, didn't you?"

It was Carlyle's turn to look surprised. "Is that truly what you think? Is that truly what *he* thinks? Your father was a good copper, Erin O'Reilly. He was never on the take, which is more than can be said of a great many patrolmen, even in these enlightened days. I respected him. He'd gotten himself into a bad position, through no fault of his own, and I was in a position to assist. If any ordinary citizen had done the same thing, you'd be hailing him as a hero."

"You're no ordinary citizen!" she burst out. "You're a goddamn gangster! And so is he!"

"Here now," Corky said. "What exactly are you saying, Erin?"

"You knew I was a detective," she said, and to her horror she felt angry tears threatening to spill out of her eyes. She was afraid he'd see them and think she was being weak, when they were really just overflowing rage. "You were using me! Is that what you do? Just screw your way onto the good side of any female cop who comes around?"

"Erin, I didn't care you were a copper," Corky said, and he actually looked hurt at her accusation. "I thought you were lovely, surely. I knew you were tough, and I liked that. I thought you knew who I was. Surely you did your homework before coming to the Corner? Half the lads in this place have been connected at one time or another. There's coppers who come in here, too. Any of them could have told you."

"You may not care I'm a cop," she said. "But I damn well care you're a gangster."

"Romeo and Juliet, is that it?" he asked with a lopsided smile. "Star-crossed lovers?"

Erin snorted in exasperation and turned away from him, distracted by motion at the entrance to the bar. A FedEx guy was wheeling in a package. It was a black plastic carrying case with a built-in wheel assembly. Danny came out from behind the bar to sign for it. She turned her attention back to the men in front of her.

"Do you have any idea what would happen to my career?" she demanded. "If it came out I was messing around with a member of the Irish mob?"

Carlyle nodded absently and glanced at Danny. "What've we got there, lad?" he asked.

"Case of Glen D, boss," Danny called back. "We were down one in the last shipment. It's to make up the shortfall."

"Grand," Carlyle said, not giving his bartender his full attention. He was watching his best friend and that friend's not-quite-girlfriend.

"It needn't be a problem," Corky said. "As long as we're discreet."

"Do you even know what that word means?" she asked in disbelief.

He grinned. "I've heard of it. Thought I might give it a try one of these days."

Rolf, uninterested in the human argument, was keeping an eye on Danny as he hefted the whiskey case onto the bar and checked the invoice. The dog walked to the end of his leash and sat, holding perfectly still and staring at the bartender.

At that moment Erin's phone buzzed in her pocket. She was just getting set to really rip into Corky, but she was also technically on duty. She fished out the phone, holding up a hand in his face, index finger raised, a clear signal that she wasn't done with him yet.

"O'Reilly," she answered.

"Erin? Skip here," the bomb-squad technician said. "Great collar. I'm at the Fergus place now, checking things over."

"Okay, sure," she said. "Look, Skip, I'm kind of in the middle of something. What's up?"

She felt like too many things were jostling for her attention. Corky, Carlyle, the call from the office, her dog, whatever was going on at the bar, her own emotions. She still had adrenaline lingering from the shootout, giving little alarms of danger. She was jumpy as hell.

"I've just taken inventory at Fergus's lab," Skip said. He didn't sound quite like his usual cheery, friendly self. "Erin, there's not enough chemicals. He made at least one bomb, and it's not here."

Time slowed down as all the pieces fell into place. Rolf hadn't been given an order, but he was a pretty smart dog, and this time he was working as a free agent. He was sitting in a perfect alert posture, just like he was supposed to. And Danny had just unsnapped the catches on the lid of the carrying case.

The cell phone dropped out of Erin's hand, forgotten. She had time to get out maybe one word before everything went to hell. "Bomb!" she screamed.

Most people would have frozen at that word. But Danny was already flipping open the lid. And Carlyle and Corky had grown up in Belfast during the Troubles. For them, a bomb threat wasn't theoretical. Carlyle flung himself on top of Erin, even as she dove for the floor. And Corky, moving with his unearthly reflexes, sprang across the room, thrusting his hands at the package even as Danny instinctively recoiled, arms coming up in front of his face.

There was a flat, metallic snap, a yelp of surprise and pain from Corky, and then silence.

Erin was pressed flat to the floor of the pub, Carlyle lying on top of her. "Carlyle," she said, her voice muffled by his sport coat.

"You all right?" he asked.

"Yeah," she said. "Get off."

"Is *she* all right?" Corky repeated in a quiet, tight voice.

"Corks?" Carlyle asked, rolling off Erin. The two of them cautiously rose to their feet. Corky was standing at the bar, one hand inside the box, the other holding the lid halfway open. The muscles on his jaw and neck were so clenched they quivered visibly. He was trying with every bit of his self-control to hold perfectly still.

"Corky," Erin said, doing her best to keep her own voice steady. "Don't move an inch."

The Irishman actually smiled through his tension. "Now just where would I be bloody well going?"

Erin fumbled on the floor for her dropped phone, keeping her eyes on Corky. "Danny? Get outside right now," she said. "Get everyone back, away from the building."

"She's right, Danny," Carlyle said. "We'll be fine. Go."

The bartender, eyes wide, nodded and hurried out of the pub, followed by the waitress and the other patrons.

"Speak for yourselves," Corky said. "I'm the one with my bloody hand in a bloody bomb."

"Rolf, *raus!*" she ordered, pointing. "Danny? Take him clear of here." The dog was confused, but orders were orders. He trotted out of the Corner behind the bartender, the door swinging shut behind them.

"Erin? You there? Everything okay?" Skip's voice came through the phone.

"Yeah, Skip," she said. "We have a situation here. I'm at the

Barley Corner. I think we've found your bomb."

"Okay, great!" Skip said. "I'll be right there. Don't touch it. Get everyone out."

She closed her eyes. "It's a little late for that. We've got a guy holding it right now, and I think it's armed."

"Jesus Christ," the bomb tech said. He put his hand over the phone and snapped some orders to the rest of his squad, then came back on the line. "We're rolling. Get the hell out of there. Tell your guy to stay calm. Five, ten minutes tops, we're there."

Erin turned to Corky. To her disbelief, Carlyle was walking toward his friend. "Get away from him!" she snapped. "You want to get killed?"

Carlyle ignored her. "What've we got?" he asked Corky calmly.

"Something bit my hand," Corky said. "I'm thinking it's a rat-trap. Snapped right on my fingernails, hurts like a bloody bastard."

"The bomb squad's on its way," Erin said. "Just hold still, five minutes."

Corky's smile was a little shaky. "I'll try, love," he said. "But I'm not sure I can manage it."

Erin's anger had been buried under a wave of renewed adrenaline and professionalism. "You're gonna be okay," she said. Disregarding her own and Skip's advice, she closed the distance to the man. "We're gonna get you out of this."

"Dammit, Erin," Skip said. In the background on the line she heard car doors slamming and an engine starting up. "Get clear!"

"Can't do that, Skip," she said, taking a close look at Corky. His arms were trembling slightly and sweat was running down his face. His posture was an awkward half-crouch, his hands extended, left hand on the lid of the case, right hand inside. He wasn't going to be able to hold it much longer. "We're gonna have to try to disarm it now."

"Shit," Skip said. "Who's there with you?"

"Two wiseguys," she said. "James Corcoran's got his hand on the bomb, Morton Carlyle's here too."

"Cars Carlyle? Good. Great. Put him on."

"I'll put you on speaker," she said, touching the screen and setting the phone on the bar.

"Cars?" Skip called.

"Right here," Carlyle said softly. He was bent over, staring into the case. "Erin? If you'd be so kind, there's a flashlight under the bar, by the register."

She scrambled around the bar, found a flashlight, and handed it across the bar. Carlyle flicked it on and looked past Corky's arm.

"Skip Taylor, NYPD bomb squad," the tech introduced himself. "It's probably a nitro bomb, homemade, unstable."

"Grand," Carlyle said. "I see a wire strung to the lid, attached to a rat-trap. The trap's taped to the foam packing. There's six bottles inside."

"Okay, the nitro's going to be in the bottles," Skip said. "It's a carrying case of some sort?"

"Aye," Carlyle said. "Wine case, for transporting glass bottles."

"Okay," Skip said. "So there's an open circuit. The metal of the trap connects, it completes the circuit, and boom."

"That's my thinking," Carlyle agreed.

"Have you got wire-cutters?"

"Aye, in the cellar," Carlyle said. "But we've no time to fetch them. How far out are you?"

"Goddamn traffic," Skip said. "Another six, seven minutes."

"No good," Erin said.

"I've a knife in my pocket," Corky said.

"Which one?" Erin asked.

"Right hip."

"I'll get it." Erin moved around behind him. "Hold still." She eased a hand into his pocket and felt a handle.

"Well, Erin," Corky said. "After the way our conversation started, I didn't think you'd be putting a hand on me there."

"Shut up," she said. She pulled out a spring-loaded OTF Scarab knife from the pocket and flicked the switch, extending a three-and-a-half-inch double-edged blade. "Nice knife. What'd it set you back?"

"A good thousand. It doesn't pay to skimp on quality for this sort of thing. Careful; it's fresh-sharpened."

"Okay, Skip, I've got a knife," Erin said.

"That should do well," Carlyle said.

"Can you see an anti-tampering device?" Skip asked.

"Nay," Carlyle said, staring hard into the gap between lid and case. "This is a homemade device, nothing fancy. If we cut the wire, it should deactivate the trigger."

"Okay," Skip said.

"This is beginning to hurt more than a little," Corky commented, still trying to keep his voice light and cheerful.

"I can get my hand in there, put something in place of your finger," Erin said.

"Is there any slack on the lid?" Skip asked.

Carlyle panned the flashlight. "Nay," he sighed. "There's a second wire."

"Not a good idea, Erin," Skip said. "Don't jostle the lid. Everyone just relax and move slow."

"If the trap's already been sprung, why can't you open the lid the rest of the way?" Erin asked.

"There's a fail-safe," the Irish bomb-maker explained. "I think the second wire is a manual trigger. I don't know how much give it has without opening the box, which renders the point rather moot, as that will trigger the bomb."

"You have to cut the manual-trigger wire, and the wire from

the trap to the detonator," Skip said.

"You're right," Carlyle said. "But my hand's too large for the space."

"I can manage it," Corky said.

"No," Erin said. "You might move your other hand. I've got the smallest hands. I'll do it."

"You certain?" Carlyle asked. "How steady can you be?"

She looked down and saw no tremor in her fingers. "I've got this," she said, feeling oddly calm. The shakes would come later, assuming she survived. "Hold the light and tell me what to cut."

"All right," Carlyle said. "You see the wire wrapped about the baseplate of the trap?"

"Yeah." It was a thin copper wire, shining bright and new in the flashlight beam.

"You need to cut that wire. But be very careful not to touch the blade to the arm of the trap when you do it."

"That'll complete the circuit," Skip said, adding unnecessarily, "You don't wanna do that."

"Once you've cut that wire, there's another to the left side there," Carlyle said. "You have to cut that one, too."

Erin nodded. She took a slow, deep breath, and eased the knife into the case. She tried not to think about the fact that her hand was hovering above a very large amount of powerful homemade explosive. She understood now why Skip didn't like wearing the bomb suit. If she screwed up, she thought, they could forget about open versus closed casket; they'd be burying an empty one.

Corky's breath was coming in shaky gasps. "I think... my nail's tearing," he muttered. "Bloody trap's.... cutting through the middle. If the nail goes, that's all she... bloody well wrote."

"Hold on," Erin said. The knife was a little over eight inches long all told, and was tricky to maneuver. She had it inside the case, but was having trouble getting the blade into the right place.

"When we... get out of this," Corky said, "what do you say... to another drink?"

"Corky, just because I grabbed your ass doesn't make us a couple," she said, trying to keep him distracted. "I'm still pissed at you."

"I'm sorry... about the confusion... regarding my occupa-tion," he said. "Still, they say... tense situations... bring people closer."

"Is he always like this?" Erin asked Carlyle. The tip of the knife snagged in the packaging foam for a moment, but the sharp blade sliced clear of it. It clinked against one of the bottles for a heart-stopping moment, but again nothing happened.

"You've no idea," Carlyle said. "In all my time with the Brigades, I never knew a one like him for encouraging the patriotism of Irish lasses."

Erin felt the blade scrape against the copper wire. "You failed to mention that," she said to Corky, gritted her teeth, and cut the wire.

There was a breathless moment. "Got it," she said.

"Now the other one," Carlyle said. "You're doing grand."

Sirens were audible, rapidly closing. Erin hardly heard them. She saw the other wire, anchoring the lid of the box, and slashed across with the knife. Corky was right. The Scarab's double-edged blade was as sharp as anything she'd ever held. It went through the wire with no resistance at all.

Carlyle took hold of the handle on top of the lid and opened it, revealing the interior of the case. He grabbed a packet of napkins off the bar and thrust a folded bundle into the rat-trap beside his friend's fingers. Corky jerked his hand free of the trap and sank onto a bar stool, cradling his injured hand.

"Clear," Erin said, stepping back from the bomb.

She heard Skip's sigh of relief. "Okay, good work, Erin," he said. "Now will you please listen to the expert and get the hell away from the bomb?"

Chapter 17

An unbelievable number of police officers descended on the Barley Corner. Since the bomb was still technically armed, everyone had to evacuate to a safe distance. Unfortunately, since no one knew exactly how powerful the device was, this meant setting up a perimeter a full block away, evacuating the surrounding buildings, and generally screwing up the day of everyone in the neighborhood.

Skip Taylor arrived before the exodus had really gotten started. He didn't bother with the bomb suit. He just walked into the pub like any customer, examined the device, pronounced it safe, then had to wait anyway while the evacuation proceeded. Protocols had to be observed, and some bureaucrat had decided not to believe the guy who'd deactivated IEDs on a daily basis in Iraq.

"Is this Don't Listen to Skip day?" he grumbled to Erin as they watched uniformed officers sweeping the block. "Hell, I could;ve *built* a damn bomb by now.."

"How dangerous is it?" she asked. Rolf was back at her side, Danny having handed the leash to her as soon as she'd left the pub.

"I wouldn't want to drop it," he said. "But otherwise, it's no big deal. I'll need to take it apart to make sure, but it looked like three bottles of nitro, a road flare rigged to the detonator, and two bundles of roofing nails."

Erin couldn't suppress a shudder. "What sort of damage would that do?"

He shrugged. "It would've wiped out the bar," he said. "Killed everyone in the place, everyone upstairs. The windows would've been gone for sure, which would've propelled broken plate glass, bottle glass, and nails on the blast wave, taken out everyone for oh, thirty or forty yards at least. Maybe more. Depends how good a job our guy did mixing the stuff. If it's pure? The building would've probably come down."

Erin shivered again, sorry she'd asked. "Skip, I had my *hands* in that box."

He scratched the back of his head. "See, that's why you gotta listen to the bomb-squad guy."

"O'Reilly!"

The shout was like the voice of God, if God smoked too many cigarettes and needed to go to anger-management therapy. Erin took a deep breath, squared her shoulders, and turned to face Lieutenant Webb.

Erin's CO was coming down the street toward her, fists clenched. The rest of the Major Crimes squad hung back a little, letting their boss take the lead.

"Here, sir," she said wearily. She suddenly felt unbelievably tired, as the effects of adrenaline leaked out of her. Every muscle was sore. She stood at attention the best she could.

"I don't know how you did things down in Queens, but here in the big city, we don't practice disarming bombs by ourselves, without even telling our squad-mates where we are!" Webb was right up in her face, flushed and furious. "Do you *want* to get killed? Do you want a transfer? Because it's against departmental policy to kill you, but I can absolutely toss you back on Patrol so fast your head will spin!"

"Sir..." Erin began.

"Jesus Christ!" Webb shouted. "You could've blown up the whole block! When you found out about the bomb, did it ever cross your mind that maybe, just *maybe* you ought to talk to someone before running off on your own?"

"I didn't know about the bomb," Erin interrupted.

"You what?" Webb stopped mid-rant. "What do you mean, you didn't know about it?"

"The FedEx guy dropped it off in the middle of things," she said.

"Then why... what the hell were you doing there in the first place?"

That wasn't a question Erin wanted to answer. She tried to come up with something that wouldn't be a lie. "I was looking into a connection of Mr. Carlyle's. I thought maybe there was some information I needed that I hadn't gotten."

Webb rubbed his temples. "God damn it, O'Reilly. You are either the luckiest or the unluckiest cop in the Five Boroughs." He turned and waved the other members of the squad over. "Come on, circle up, people."

Jones and Vic cautiously approached.

"Okay, everyone. Let's talk this through. I want to know exactly what happened. Who did what to whom, and what can we prove?"

Erin glanced at the other two. Jones raised an eyebrow and gestured for her to go ahead.

"It's like this, sir," Erin began. "Billy O'Connell had a problem. He loved to gamble, but Fourth-Place Billy just couldn't pick winners. He got in the hole, pretty deep. I'm guessing he worked with multiple bookies so he could run up a bigger tab. Anyway, he owed Morton Carlyle and Franklin

Fergus. It was Frankie who gave him the solution to his problem.

"At first it was just working off the debt doing collections. But O'Connell wasn't really cut out for it. He started carrying a gun, sure, but he wasn't a scary enough guy. Frankie had men who'd do that kind of work for him, guys like Knox and Morgan. Those boys had records and were willing to put the hurt on people. O'Connell needed something better.

"Fergus gave him the idea of offing his wife for the insurance money. Make it look like a mob hit on O'Connell himself. Who'd suspect a guy who'd barely escaped being a victim? It must've seemed perfect to Fergus. He'd clear a debt off his books, he'd graduate one of his enforcers to the next level, with perfect blackmail leverage, and he could even pin the crime on his rival, Carlyle.

"I think when we look into gambling in this neighborhood, we're gonna find that Carlyle and Fergus are working a lot of the same territory, and that doesn't lead to friendly relations. O'Connell might not have known Fergus was planning to pin the whole thing on Carlyle, but I'm guessing he did. After all, if Cars went upstate, O'Connell wouldn't have to worry about those debts, either."

Erin paused, looking for confirmation. Her colleagues were listening. Jones was nodding. Vic ran a hand over his knuckles and smiled thinly.

"Go on, Detective," Webb said.

"Then O'Connell screwed it up. He botched the bomb. It was nitroglycerin, really unstable stuff, and he was an amateur. Instead of taking out his wife, O'Connell managed to assassinate himself. Fergus didn't care too much. Sure, he wouldn't collect on the debt, but at least he could still frame Carlyle and come out ahead. He played hard to get, then he and his guys tossed Carlyle to us in interrogation.

"But Vic and I figured the frame-up job and went after Fergus. Unfortunately, Frankie had already decided we weren't going to stick Carlyle with the car bomb. I don't know how he was planning to play it; probably try to pass it off as some other mob making a move on the Irish. If I had to guess, knowing how this guy operates, I'd say he was going to fake an attempt on his own life, too, to throw off suspicion, while Carlyle would still get blown up.

"Fortunately, Skip found the missing bomb materials at Fergus's place and called me. And my partner," she scratched Rolf behind the ears, "sniffed out the bomb just in time. One of Carlyle's guys, Corcoran, managed to get his hand on the trigger and keep it from going off. Then Skip walked Carlyle and me through disarming it."

"Okay," Webb said. His face had returned to its normal color, and he didn't sound pissed off anymore. "Good summation. So, what can we make stick?"

"We can match the bomb chemicals to the lab at Fergus's place," Jones said. "That gives us attempted murder and attempted use of a weapon of mass destruction. Everything else is just icing on that, but if we want, we can stick him with obstruction of justice for his false testimony, resisting arrest, conspiracy to commit murder for trying to do in Mrs. O'Connell, and if we can match chemicals with O'Connell's bomb lab to Fergus's lab, we've probably got him on Murder One for O'Connell."

"He could bargain that one down to manslaughter," Vic said, "on account of how O'Connell wasn't supposed to die in the first place." He grinned. "Not that it'll do him much good. Might take one lifetime off his sentence."

"With attempted murder of police officers hanging over Knox and Morgan, they'll flip easy," Jones went on. "We've got them cold on that. Fingerprints on their guns."

"Okay, that sorts Fergus's gang," Webb said. "What about Carlyle?"

"What about him, sir?" Erin asked, startled.

"What've we got on him?"

"Um," she said. "Well, there's the gambling. If we can prove any of it goes through him directly. But he didn't actually build any of these bombs. He even helped defuse the one that came to the Corner. If anything, he's... well, he's an intended victim. Maybe even a hero. Sort of."

Webb actually laughed quietly at that. "I'll be damned," he said. "But he's no hero. We'll pick him up another time."

"Yes, sir," Erin said, with the unspoken thought that Carlyle had proven pretty hard to catch in the past.

A Patrol Lieutenant approached Skip, who was nonchalantly leaning against the outside wall of the Corner. "We're clear, Sergeant Taylor," he said.

"Thank God," Skip said. "You do know that nitroglycerin gets more unstable over time, right? It sweats. The chemicals start breaking down, crystals form, it can go off for no reason at all."

"Really?" the other cop said, taking a step backward. "I'll just... uh... wait down the block." He hurried away.

Skip turned to the detectives with a grin. "Guess I'll go get your bomb."

"Is that true, what you just told him?" Erin asked.

"Of course it is," he said. "But it takes about a year for the sweating to be a serious problem." He winked. "Oh, Erin? Could I talk to you a second?"

"Sure." She followed him a short distance inside. "What is it?"

"So, who's this Corky character?" he asked. "And why does he think you're a couple?"

Erin opened her mouth and realized she had no idea what to

say.

Skip grinned. "Never mind. Sorry I asked."

Erin left him to his cleanup work and rejoined the other detectives.

"All right, team," Webb said. "*Now* I think we can call this case closed."

"Except for the paperwork, sir," Jones said. "There's going to be a lot of that."

Vic groaned. "Is it too late to just set off the bomb instead? With me beside it?"

Chapter 18

Erin O'Reilly took an extra moment to look over her desk. She saw clutter, but it was semi-organized clutter, the look of a workspace with a lot going on. She stood up and stretched. Rolf sprang up from the floor mat she'd laid next to the desk, tail wagging.

"Quitting time," Jones said. She was shutting down her own computer and getting ready to leave.

"Yeah," Vic said. "But it's Friday, remember. Everyone else gets the weekend off. The NYPD never closes. Lots of murders on the weekend."

"Mondays are the worst day for workplace killings," Jones said. "Statistically speaking."

"I'm not surprised," Vic said.

"On that note," Webb said, "you're off until Monday, right, O'Reilly?"

"Yes, sir."

"Guess we may have some work for you when you get back," he said.

Erin clipped on Rolf's leash and headed down to the parking garage. She and her partner got into her Charger and drove out onto the street.

The rest of the week was quiet. They hadn't caught another major case, so there'd been plenty of time to deal with the aftermath of the bomb plots. As predicted, Morgan and Knox had both turned on their boss in exchange for plea deals, and Erin didn't think Frankie Fingers would be hitting the streets again. Not with the number of felony counts stacked up against him.

Cynthia O'Connell hadn't come out very well. True to form, William O'Connell's life-insurance company was refusing to pay out his policy, citing the suicide clause. Even in death, Fourth-Place Billy just couldn't catch a break. At least Cynthia was free of a husband who, in addition to being a compulsive gambler and aspiring mob thug, had tried to murder her. And her flowers were doing very well, as she'd told Erin when they'd given her the news of the closure of her husband's investigation. There was a show this weekend. She hoped her damask roses would win first prize.

Erin shook her head and smiled to herself. What she was doing was probably stupid, but she couldn't really help herself. She had to look in at the Barley Corner one more time, see how the Irish were handling themselves. Plus, it'd been a long week, she needed a drink, and it was as good a place as any to get one.

It was a Friday evening and the place was hopping. Ninety percent of the clientele were large, male, tattooed, and inebriated, but Rolf helped her clear a path to the bar. There was Carlyle, in his usual spot, seated on a stool with his back to the bar, elbows resting on the well-worn wood. And beside him sat his best mate, Corky Corcoran.

Carlyle didn't miss any new arrival to his pub. His face lit up with a smile that looked truly genuine. "Erin O'Reilly!" he exclaimed, rising to his feet. "What a grand surprise. Welcome!" He extended one hand to the bartender. "Anything you might be wanting, tell Danny. It's on the house."

"In a minute," she said, sliding into a seat that had become available by some sort of unspoken communication between Carlyle and its former occupant. "Looks like the bomb scare hasn't done your business any harm."

"You must be joking," Corky said. "It's been packing the lads in. I'll be drinking on that story for years to come. It's not every lad has had a nail-bomb in his hands, and saved a sweet lass from a terrible fate."

Erin chuckled. "The way I remember it, the sweet lass saved the reckless lad from a terrible fate, not the other way round."

"Either way," Corky said with a grin. "Erin, love, you're surely not angry with me anymore, are you?"

To her surprise, she found that she wasn't. "You're incorrigible," she said. "But no, I'm not pissed. You were just being yourself."

"That's true enough," Corky said agreeably. "So, what do you say to a drink, and then go dancing with me?"

Erin shook her head. "No, Corky," she said. "I really don't think it'd work out. You do what you do, and I do what I do. Besides, you're not a keeper."

"Maybe not," he said. "But it might be fun to have me around for a while, don't you think?"

"It'd certainly be interesting," she said. "But I think we'd better just be friends."

"Friends?" Corky said. "Aye. You can't be friends with too many coppers, that's my way of thinking." He held out his hand.

Erin rolled her eyes. "Don't read too much into it. You step over the line, I'll still be there slapping the cuffs on you."

"Promises, promises," he said with an even broader grin. "I may hold you to that, one of these days."

"In all seriousness, Miss O'Reilly... may I call you Erin?" Carlyle said.

"We disarmed a bomb together," she said. "Why not?"

"Erin, then. It's thanks to you my place of business survives. More than that, I think I owe you my life."

She shook her head. "It's my job."

"Call it what you like," he replied. "You've done me a favor I'll not find it easy to repay."

A little warning bell went off in Erin's brain. "Your world runs on favors, Cars," she said. "Mine doesn't."

"You might be surprised," Carlyle replied, with no humor in his eyes. "And you might be surprised how useful a lass in your line of work might find a lad in mine. Should that prove the case, you've only to call on me."

He was right, Erin knew. Underworld contacts could be worth their weight in gold to a detective. She still didn't feel comfortable around him, but she couldn't deny that she liked and trusted him more than she had before. Probably more than she should.

"I'll keep that in mind," she said.

"All right, then," Carlyle said. "That's settled. Now, is there any other business you've come about?"

"No," she said. "I just wanted to make sure no one else had blown up your pub."

"Then you're off-duty," he said.

"Yeah."

"Surely you'd not refuse a drink with us, then," he said. "A toast for those who cheated the Reaper?"

"Why the hell not," she said.

Danny appeared, using that strange ability of a good bartender to know when a patron was ready to order. "What'll it be?" he asked.

What else? Erin thought. "Gimme a car bomb."

Danny blinked. "Excuse me?"

Carlyle and Corky laughed. "Make it two," Carlyle said.

"Three," Corky added.

Danny poured three glasses of Guinness, half-filled three shot glasses with Glen D whiskey, then floated Irish cream on top of them. He dropped them one, two, three into the beer glasses. "Bombs away," he said.

"Here's to the New York Police Department, and its finest new detective," Carlyle said.

"And to the Irish, without whom New York wouldn't have a police force," Erin said.

"And without whom it wouldn't need one," Corky added.

They clinked glasses, tilted them back, and drank.

Here's a sneak peek from Book 3: White Russian

Coming Winter 2018

Vic and Erin rode to the motel together in Erin's Charger, Rolf in his back-seat compartment. They crossed the East River into Brooklyn on the famous bridge. Erin shook her head and stifled a laugh.

"What's funny?" Vic asked.

"I just finished moving into Manhattan," she said. "Now, my first night in my new place, and I'm spending it in Brooklyn. Not my idea of a celebration."

"Maybe we'll still have time for that drink," Vic said. "After."

It was full dark by the time they got to the motel. They

knew the place before they even got close, from all the red and blue lights. It looked like seven or eight units had already responded. There was an ambulance, too, but as they pulled up they could see the paramedics leaning on the back fender looking bored. That wasn't a good sign.

Webb's Crown Victoria was in the lot, too. Erin saw the Lieutenant talking to a couple of uniforms outside the lobby. She hopped out of the Charger, fetched Rolf, and headed over to her CO.

"What's the situation, sir?" she asked.

"I see you brought Neshenko," Webb said. "Good." He looked even wearier and more cynical than usual. He had an unlit cigarette in one hand, forgotten. "I just talked to the ME. She's on her way, should be here in ten to fifteen."

He sighed. "It's bad. We've got two victims, DOA. The medics didn't even bother trying to patch them up. The night manager heard gunfire. She thought it was a movie at first, until she heard the screaming and bullets came through the wall into the hallway." He jerked a thumb in the direction of the lobby. A young woman was sitting in a chair next to a uniformed officer. The woman was crying. "It's a ground-floor room, number 103," he went on. "Jones is there now, securing the scene."

"Okay, let's check it out," Erin said.

Webb nodded. "Carefully, people." They crossed the lobby into the hallway.

"Good thing nobody was walking here," Vic observed. The wall to their right was riddled with holes. Chunks of plaster and ribbons of cheap wallpaper were scattered all over the floor.

"Hey, guys. Took your time getting here." Kira Jones waved from the doorway of room 103. She was dressed for a night on the town, from her high-heeled boots and miniskirt to her spiked hair, which was dyed dark red with blue tips. Erin had heard the precinct had a pool running on how many tattoos she had hidden under her clothes.

"Jesus, I can smell the gunpowder from here," Vic said.

"No shit," Jones said. "Have a look."

They gathered in the doorway, looking into what had been a cheap motel room. Now it was a war zone. Bullet holes were everywhere, perforating the queen-size bed and wood-veneer furniture. An uneven line of jagged holes angled across the TV screen. Cartridge casings were scattered across the carpet, most of them near the window. The window itself was shattered into tiny shards.

And there were the bodies. Two of them, a man and a woman. They lay close together, beside the bed. The man was face-down, wearing a shirt that'd been white when he'd put it on but was now dark red. He had on very nice shoes and black slacks. The woman was on her back, clad in a bright red dress that did a better job of hiding the bloodstains. One black stiletto heel was still on her foot. She'd kicked off the other shoe, maybe as a dying reflex. That shoe, lying in a dark bloodstain on the carpet, caught Erin's eye. For some reason, it was the worst detail in the room, that bare foot with the toes thrusting toward the ceiling. It was even worse than the woman's wide-open eyes, or the bullet hole in the middle of her forehead.

"Wow," Erin said.

"That's a hell of a lot of bullets," Vic said, indicating the room with a sweep of his hand.

Webb was crouching down, looking at a cartridge casing. ".45 caliber," he said.

"MAC-10?" Jones suggested.

"More than one," Erin said. There were just too many bullet holes. A MAC-10 submachine-gun could spit out plenty of lead, but it only held thirty bullets in a magazine. There were way more than thirty holes.

"I'm thinking three shooters," Vic said. "Maybe more.

Window?"

"Yeah," Erin agreed. The damage to the room was all on the half away from the window. She carefully crossed the room, avoiding stepping on any of the debris or bodies. Rolf daintily picked up his paws, sniffing at everything in his path. She leaned out the window. As she'd suspected, she saw a whole lot more cartridge casings. "Looks like they opened fire from here, through the glass," she reported.

"It wasn't a drive-by," Webb said. "They had to dismount, otherwise most of the brass would still be in the car. And with more brass inside, at least one of them climbed inside and kept shooting."

"So at least three guys come up, look in the window, and blast through it," Jones said. "Then what? They come into the room? Why?"

"They had to make sure," Erin said. She turned at the window and stared into the room, seeing how it would have looked from outside. "I can't even see the bodies from here. They fell behind the bed. Maybe they were dead, maybe not, but the shooters wouldn't have been able to tell from here."

"I got an empty mag out here," one of the uniforms said helpfully. "Looks like it came from an automatic weapon."

"Christ," Vic said. "They *reloaded*? I guess they had to. MAC-10s go through bullets like junkies through heroin."

"Okay," Erin said, walking through it. "At least one of them reloads outside. They climb in through the window, go around the foot of the bed, look down, and finish them off."

"No bullet holes in the floor," Webb pointed out. "Look at the male's position. He tried to get up and run. They gunned him down before he got to the door. I'm thinking he ducked the first volley, then got hit later."

"Right in the back," Vic said. "Bastards. Mob hit. It's gotta be. Shitty marksmanship, though, if they didn't hit him on the first try."

"Maybe he was quick," Erin said. "Or he might've gotten wounded but could still run."

Movement in the doorway caught their attention. All four detectives saw Sarah Levine, the Medical Examiner. Unlike the other investigators, she looked like she'd come straight from the precinct. She had her lab coat and gloves on, ready to do business.

"Glad we didn't wake you up," Webb said.

"Huh?" Levine asked blankly. "No, I was awake. I'm working nights this week. Where's the dead guy?"

"Her boyfriend's a doctor," Jones explained to Erin in an undertone. "She tries to coordinate schedules with him."

"She's got a boyfriend?" Erin whispered, astonished. Levine wasn't unattractive, but she was one of the most poorly-socialized women she'd ever met.

"Hey, there's someone for everyone," Jones replied with a wink.

Levine took a good, long look at the bodies.

"Got a cause of death for us, Doc?" Vic asked with a sardonic smile.

"Not yet," Levine said.

"That was a joke, Doc," Vic said. "We know the cause of death."

Levine looked up. "Okay, Detective. What killed her?"

"A whole bunch of .45 slugs," Vic said.

"No."

Vic blinked. "You telling me she was already dead? Or she died of something else? Tell you what. Maybe she had a heart attack. Or how about cancer? Really, really fast-acting cancer?"

Levine wasn't good at sarcasm. "I won't know about underlying medical conditions until I do the bloodwork and the autopsy," she said. "But I can see she's got at least three bullet wounds to her legs and lower abdomen. Those didn't kill her. What killed her is this." She took a pencil out of her lab coat's pocket and pointed to the hole in the middle of the woman's forehead.

"That's what I said," Vic said.

"You said .45 slugs killed her," Levine said. "This hole's too small for a .45. I'd say nine-millimeter."

"Nine-millimeter," Erin echoed, scanning the floor of the room. There wasn't as much spent brass in here as outside, but it still took her a minute to find the one that was different. Then she saw it. The shell casing had flown a surprising distance, ending up at the base of the TV stand. "I've got it here," she said, stooping to take a closer look. "One nine-millimeter pistol casing. Looks a little funny, though. Not quite like a standard nine."

"There's powder tattooing around the entry wound," Levine said. "The gun was almost contact close. Probably less than a meter."

"Execution style," Webb said.

"What about the guy?" Vic asked.

"He's got five shots in the back," Levine said. "Both lungs perforated, along with a heart shot. He was dead by the time he hit the ground."

"So they mowed down the guy, then took out the girl to eliminate the witness," Vic said.

"Either that, or she was the target," Erin suggested.

"She's a hooker," Webb said. "Look at the clothes."

"What's that got to do with it?" Jones retorted. "People kill hookers all the time."

"Prostitutes get knifed or beaten to death," Webb said. "Not blown away with machine guns. Ten bucks says when we ID this guy, he's gonna be a mobster."

"No bet," Vic said.

"I'll take some of that action," Erin said. She was staring at the young face of the woman—more of a girl, really. "I got ten says you're wrong, sir."

Ready for more?

Join Steven Henry's author email list
for the latest on new releases, upcoming books and
series, behind-the-scenes details, events, and more.

Be the first to know about new releases in the Erin
O'Reilly Mysteries by signing up at
tinyurl.com/StevenHenryEmail

Acknowledgments

It'd be nice to be able to say I wrote and published this book all by myself. But the truth is even better. This book exists because of friends, family, and colleagues who believed in the story, and in me.

First, there's Ben Faroe of Clickworks Press, who has devoted a great deal of time to editing, assisting with promotion, and all the gritty little details of actually getting this book from my brain into your hands. Thank you, Ben and Kristen, for your support.

Thank you to the Burnsville, MN Police Department and their Citizens' Academy program. Thanks to you, I know a lot more about what it's like to wear a shield. Stay safe out there. You're doing a great job!

A big thank-you to my first-draft readers: Carl and Mary Caroline Henry, Dave and Marilyn Lindstrom, and Kira Woodmansee. A first draft is a good start, but it's a long way from finished. Thank you for your moral support and initial feedback.

I'd be remiss if I didn't give credit to Shelley Paulson for my author photo. She made me look better on the page than I do in real life.

Particular thanks go to my PI roleplaying group, for your

character creation and interactions. This book is based on one of the first of our adventures together. I hope I've done well rewriting and adapting it to the page. David Greenfield, Justin Moor, Hilary and Mark Murphy, Bridget Johnson, and Ben Lurie, you made it possible, and you made it fun.

Last on the list, and first in my heart, is my wife Ingrid, who first came up with Erin O'Reilly and brought her to life. You are a constant encouragement and inspiration to me, listening to my rough-copy, brainstorming ideas, and never giving up on me.

About the Author

Steven Henry learned how to read almost before he learned how to walk. Ever since he began reading stories, he wanted to put his own on the page. He lives a very quiet and ordinary life in Minnesota with his wife and dog.

Also by Steven Henry

Ember of Dreams
The Clarion Chronicles, Book One

When magic awakens a long-forgotten folk, a noble lady, a young apprentice, and a solitary blacksmith band together to prevent war and seek understanding between humans and elves.

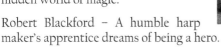

Lady Kristyn Tremayne – An otherwise unremarkable young lady's open heart and inquisitive mind reveal a hidden world of magic.

Robert Blackford – A humble harp maker's apprentice dreams of being a hero.

Master Gabriel Zane – A master blacksmith's pursuit of perfection leads him to craft an enchanted sword, drawing him out of his isolation and far from his cozy home.

Lord Luthor Carnarvon – A lonely nobleman with a dark past has won the heart of Kristyn's mother, but at what cost?

Readers love *Ember of Dreams*

"The more I got to know the characters, the more I liked them. The female lead in particular is a treat to accompany on her journey from ordinary to extraordinary."

"The author's deep understanding of his protagonists' motivations and keen eye for psychological detail make Robert and his companions a likable and memorable cast."

Learn more at tinyurl.com/emberofdreams.

More great titles from Clickworks Press

www.clickworkspress.com

Hubris Towers: The Complete First Season
Ben Y. Faroe & Bill Hoard

Comedy of manners meets comedy of errors in a new series for fans of Fawlty Towers and P. G. Wodehouse.

"So funny and endearing"

"Had me laughing so hard that I had to put it down to catch my breath"

"Astoundingly, outrageously funny!"

Learn more at clickworkspress.com/hts01.

The Dream World Collective
Ben Y. Faroe

Five friends quit their jobs to chase what they love. Rent looms. Hilarity ensues.

"If you like interesting personalities, hidden depths... and hilarious dialog, this is the book for you."

"a fun, inspiring read—perfect for a sunny summer day."

"a heartwarming, feel-good story"

Learn more at clickworkspress.com/dwc.

Death's Dream Kingdom
Gabriel Blanchard

A young woman of Victorian London has been transformed into a vampire. Can she survive the world of the immortal dead— or perhaps, escape it?

"The wit and humor are as Victorian as the setting... a winsomely vulnerable and tremendously crafted work of art."

"A dramatic, engaging novel which explores themes of death, love, damnation, and redemption."

Learn more at clickworkspress.com/ddk.

Share the love!

Join our microlending team at kiva.org/team/clickworkspress.

Keep in touch!

Join the Clickworks Press email list and get freebies, production updates, special deals, behind-the-scenes sneak peeks, and more.

Sign up today at clickworkspress.com/join.